S0-BCZ-005

WHEN OUR LOVE IS CHARITY

Chiara Lubich

WHEN OUR LOVE IS CHARITY
Spiritual Writings, Volume 2

New City Press

BV
4639
. L8
1991

Published in the United States by New City Press
206 Skillman Avenue, Brooklyn, New York, 11211
©1991 New City Press, New York

Translated by the New City Press editorial staff
from the original Italian
La Carità Come Ideale (©1971)
Dove Due o Più (©1976)
Gesù nel Fratello (©1978)
©Città Nuova Editrice, Rome, Italy

Cover design by Nick Cianfarani

Library of Congress Cataloging-in-Publication Data:

Lubich, Chiara, 1920-
    [Prose works.   English.   Selections]
    When our love is charity / Chiara Lubich.
        p.   cm. -- (Spiritual writings ; v. 2)
    Translated from Italian.
    Contents: When our love is charity -- Jesus in our midst -- When
did we see you Lord?
    ISBN 0-911782-93-1 : $8.95
    1. Love--Religious aspects--Christianity.   2. Jesus Christ--Person
and offices.   3. Christian life--Catholic authors.   4. Focolare
Movement.   I. Series: Lubich, Chiara, 1920- Prose works.
English.   Selections ; v. 2.
BX2350.2.L7762513   vol. 2
[BV4639]
248.4'82 s--dc20
[248.4'82]   91-25791

Scripture quotations are from *The New American Bible*
©1970 Confraternity of Christian Doctrine

Printed in the United States of America

CONTENTS

FOREWORD

Chiara Lubich is a prominent figure in ecumenism and in the growing dialogue between the world's great religions. Her own experience of life coincides with the founding and development of the Focolare movement extended throughout the world and whose spiritual basis and inspiration lies principally in the prayer of Jesus, "may they all be one" (Jn 17:21).

In 1977 she was awarded the Templeton Prize for progress of religion. She is a member of the Pontifical Council of the Laity and participated as an observer in the 1985 Synod of Bishops on the Second Vatican Council as well as the 1987 Synod on the vocation and mission of the laity. On this latter occasion she delivered an address outlining the spiritualities of the numerous ecclesial movements that have recently risen within the Church.

Since publishing her first book in 1959, entitled *Meditations,* Chiara Lubich has written extensively on a variety of spiritual topics drawn from the gospel message and in a particular way seen from the angle of unity. Since the list of her works continually increases, we thought it now useful to composite them into volumes. *A Call to Love,* the first of this set features *Our Yes to God, The Word of Life* and *The Eucharist.*

This second volume of spiritual writings binds together three of her previous works. *When Our Love is Charity* examines love and the precedence it must take in the lives of Christians. It emphasizes mutual love as expressed by Jesus in his new commandment. *Jesus in Our Midst* focuses on the spiritual yet real presence of Christ in the community. In harmony with Vatican II and the thoughts of the recent popes it brings into focus once again a truth that has hardly influenced theological and spiritual

7

thought since the time of the Church Fathers. *When Did We See You, Lord?* in the words of John Cardinal Cody, "invites us to enter upon a divine adventure—to rediscover the profound power of the gospel, to thrill to the love of God all about us, to marvel at the presence of Jesus in our brothers and sisters." Throughout these works, along with recounting her own experience, the author often quotes the saints, the popes, and the Fathers of the Church.

The Editor

PART I

WHEN OUR LOVE IS CHARITY

WHEN OUR LOVE IS CHARITY

The new humanism

The world today, influenced by conflicting philosophies, is moving toward a new kind of humanism. The human person is at the center of all thought; the human person has become a principle of attention. This progress toward a revitalized humanism is following an irreversible direction. Attentive to the signs of the times, the Church is seeking to make Christians increasingly aware of who the human person is according to its point of view. This is also the historical moment in which the Focolare has taken root. We too realize that people have a very great and specific importance. Of course humankind has always been the object of Christian love in the Church's innumerable activities of caring for different needs; but for us, people are nothing less than the pathway to God. We go to God through our neighbor.

When God made us understand this, it seemed startlingly new. It appeared to be a healthy scandal at a time when many Christians seeking God often considered other people as an obstacle on the way to him. We often explained in the beginning of the Focolare that people are to us what the convent, the cloister, and the veil are to other Christians.

Together with our neighbor, we can create an oasis of the supernatural, a touch of heaven in the world. Our neighbors can also be a test for our virtue, presenting difficulties to us; in this way they become instruments in the hands of God for our purification. Love for our neighbor is the primary and best guarantee of our purity. Poverty makes sense to us only in terms of love for our neighbor. And it is only through other persons that we can obey. The thread that runs through every aspect of our life as members of this movement is the primary importance that our neighbor has for us.

But if our neighbor is the center of interest for us, what then is the specific attitude or way we Christians can approach other people and go to God through them? We all know the answer: to love others with charity.

There are many reasons which urge us to reflect about charity: first of all, because it is our specific vocation; and also because when we live in constant charity with our neighbors, we find that we are in tune with the interest and concern of the times. We find ourselves in the contemporary trend of a people moving towards a new humanism.

Furthermore, it is useful to have a clear understanding of charity because the way of love is certainly the fastest way to God, but unless it is thoroughly and correctly understood it can also be filled with dangers.

Finally, charity will keep us faithful to Christian humanism, a humanism opened up to the Absolute.

Universality of love

Charity does not have a human origin; it is of a divine nature. The consequences of this are immense and unimaginable. Because charity is different from every other kind of love, it can have an effect and an influence beyond anything else. We have, in fact, been generated by God, we are the children of God, and we love with the same love as God.

"Let us love one another; for love is of God, and he who loves is born of God and knows God" (1 Jn 4:7). God communicates this love to us in baptism through the Holy Spirit. "God's love has been poured into our hearts through the Holy Spirit" (Rom 5:5). Through this love, we become another Jesus. This is exactly what God made us understand right from the start. We wrote in 1946:

We must aim at being another Jesus. Humanity and divinity are one in Him, so we have to aim at fusing the human in us with the divine, until they are one thing. We give God our humanity so he can bring his Son to life again in us. Here on earth we have to play the part of Jesus. When we will impersonate Christ in his complete obedience to the Father, then unity is accomplished in us.

This love, which is God's very own, has certain qualities: first, it is extended toward everyone, so it is a universal love; secondly, God's love in us compels us to be the first to love. "In this is love, not that we loved God, but that he loved us and sent his Son to be the expiation for our sins" (1 Jn 4:10).

We must fix our gaze always on the one Father of so many children, and then consider all creatures as children of that one Father. Our thoughts and affections must go beyond every human limit and acquire the habit of turning constantly to this universal brotherhood in God who is our Father.

Jesus, who is our model, taught us two things, which are ultimately one, that is, to be children of our Father and to be brothers and sisters to each other.

Since the beginning of the Focolare, we have tried to be the first to love (which naturally includes loving our enemies). This idea was very strong in us and must have come either from reading the Scriptures or as a special light from God.

We can say that these two characteristics of charity, universality and being the first to love, have been the basis of the Focolare through the work of the Holy Spirit.

The object of charity

What is it that charity loves? God and people. Charity which is God in us, loves God and loves our neighbor. Charity is like a seed, dropped into our soul by God. If the soil is right and receptive, after a while the seed sends down a little root and then a little plant grows up. Charity, therefore, expresses itself in two ways: by loving God (the root) and by loving our neighbor (the plant). Of course, the root is of greater importance than the plant. As long as the root is alive there is hope for a plant, but not vice-versa, even though the plant, through its contact with the sun and with the oxygen in the air, does make its contribution to the growth of the whole.

We know that it is our love for God that urges and enables us to love our neighbor. We wanted God alone as our ideal, and God showed us what this choice implies. Love for our neighbor increases our love of God. From the beginning we noticed that after spending the whole day devoted to others we would find in the evening a recollection in God we had never experienced before. It was God paying us back for the love we had shown him in our neighbor by making us feel his presence in our soul.

The love of God and neighbor in fact are closely related. At this point we should ask ourselves: how do we love God and how do we love our neighbor? Here a distinction needs to be made, for we can make the mistake of thinking that since charity is one thing, God and our neighbor could and should be loved in the same manner. But the expression of charity toward God and toward our neighbor is very different.

The difference becomes clear not only through studying the Scriptures, but also after personal experience in these two ways of loving.

If we have lived true charity, if we love God with all our heart and have experienced the distinctive ways of loving and of being loved by him, and we happen to notice someone confusing these two kinds of love, we recognize a dangerous error and reject it instantly and utterly. We cannot tolerate any distortion, manipulation or misunderstanding of such a love because it is thereby destroyed.

Love of God

The expressions of our love for God and for our neighbor are distinctly different. We can say things to God that we cannot say to our neighbor, for instance, "We adore you." We can abandon ourselves to him. We can hope for everything from him, but "cursed is the man who trusts in man" (Jer 17:5).

We can blindly trust him, we can thank him for having created us, for making us Christians. We can ask his forgiveness for our sins and obtain it. We can expect from him the hundredfold in this life and look forward to heaven. Furthermore, the transcendent God needs no aid from us, neither bread, as our neighbor may, nor instruction. He desires the gift of our heart, our mind, our whole being, his love and life in us. With God we can establish a real relationship of charity. Pure charity is the spiritual life which culminates in the mystical life. This spiritual life is union with God and it really is the relationship of the lover with the beloved sung in the Song of Songs. Furthermore, the union that God desires between the soul and himself is a transforming union, the fusion of the soul with God.

The relationship we have with our neighbors, of course, cannot be like that. The love God wants us to have for one another is unity in distinction. In fact, Jesus could have said, "Where two or three are united in my name, I will fuse them." But he didn't say that. Instead he said, "I will be in the midst of them" (Mt 18:20). This means unity and distinction. Creatures are finite and cannot penetrate each other, but God can penetrate each.

Love of neighbor

The outstanding characteristic of love of neighbor is its concrete expression. All the works of mercy, including the spiritual ones, are concrete actions. Of course, charity toward our neighbor, though it expresses itself concretely, cancels itself out unless it is rooted in a certain spiritual attitude. When St. Paul talks about charity, he doesn't say that it means to give bread; in fact he compares giving away everything to the poor to a "clanging cymbal" (1 Cor 13:1) if the action lacks a spiritual quality that he proceeds to describe.

He insists that charity "is patient and kind; love is not jealous, or boastful; it is not arrogant or rude. Love does not insist on its own way; it is not irritable or resentful; it does not rejoice at wrong, but rejoices in the right. Love bears all things, believes all things, hopes all things, endures all things" (1 Cor 13:4-7).

How to make ourselves one

God has taught us some very deep doctrines contained in short phrases. For example, to teach us how to live charity toward our neighbor he suggested to us "to make ourselves one," in other words to empty ourselves. To make ourselves one requires being patient. When we make ourselves one, we want what is good for the other, which means an attitude far removed from being envious. To make ourselves one, we cannot be conceited or proud, because we must be empty of ourselves. There's no room for ambition or selfishness, for we can think of nothing but the other person. We are not irritable because we have to be very calm in order to make ourselves one. We don't think of wrongs, because to make ourselves one is to hope for the triumph of goodness in the other person. Becoming one means suffering, believing, putting up with everything.

To empty ourselves

To make ourselves one with someone else we cannot let ourselves think of possible answers to give or other things to do while we are listening to our neighbor with love. We have to empty ourselves completely in order to have room for the whole of our neighbor's burden, every problem and every need, just as Jesus has done.

This "becoming empty" is characteristic of a charity that wants unity. We say in the rule of the Focolare,*

> The life of union will require that the members have a very special love of Jesus in the mystery of his abandonment. He is the divine model for all those who want to make their contribution to the union of all people with God, and with one another. He is the complete expression of all deprivations, exteriorly and especially interiorly. This absolute emptying of oneself is the indispensable condition for any effort toward a supernaturally motivated union.

A characteristic of this love is that it attracts light. Jesus said, "Who loves me will be loved by my Father, and I will love him and manifest myself to him" (Jn 14:21). If we make ourselves perfectly one with the other, and have set ourselves completely aside, we learn from experience that the Holy Spirit often tells us what response to give or inspires the right action to take.

Then, the other person experiences the relief of feeling understood. He or she will then have pure eyes with which to see the things of God, will really want to know them, will be interested in the things that we are interested in. In this way we will see our numbers grow. This is what happened in the beginning without any desire of conquest. On the contrary, the mere thought of anything like apostolate just done as a job repelled us. Moreover, we will learn to act guided by light, and our experiences with people in this regard then will make it possible for us to help others who want to live this same life of charity.

To make ourselves one makes it easier for us to love everybody. We have to be able to cut loose from the worries that were confided to us by the person we have just met, so that we

---

* All references in this publication to the rule or statutes of the Focolare (approved as the Work of Mary) are made to its rule as approved by Pope John XXIII in 1962. This rule has since been revised and updated, receiving approbation by the council of the laity on June 29, 1990.

can make ourselves one with the next to come along. This is why we are always careful not to harbor in our minds and hearts any remainder of the affection or worries. Moreover, this is also a requirement for spiritual chastity.

Becoming empty and making ourselves one must be the basis of every relationship we have. It is an essential condition for unity.

Making ourselves one can be also an expression of our collective love, when we are meeting as a group with other groups. It is the frame of mind needed for any dialogue. Besides, this is precisely our vocation.

If we are not perfect at making ourselves one we will not have the light of God and any dialogue will become sterile and get nowhere. It becomes merely a conversation, or worse, a lot of empty words. To dialogue means to love. Only the Holy Spirit in us can really help us to have dialogue. Furthermore, it is only the Holy Spirit in us that can reveal to us the subtle errors that may be concealed in the most fascinating theories. Charity is a very live issue in our times, when dialogue is given such great importance.

MUTUAL LOVE

The Scriptures in our life

Recently, I read an essay on mutual love. I was especially interested in seeing how much conformity there was between the way we live and what God requires, in other words, to what extent we could call ourselves "living Scripture." Our rule in fact says that we have to walk along the way of charity in accordance with the holy Gospel.

My first impression reading this essay was that Jesus himself, who had been the Master of the first disciples, had also instructed us. I read that the love of charity was the first thing that a member of the Christian community was taught to live. For this reason John could say, "Beloved, I am writing you no new commandment, but an old commandment which you had from the beginning" (1 Jn 2:7).

It was the same way for us. Love was the first thing that we learned to live.

Some forty years ago, love was a great novelty for the Christians we knew. You could not even mention it without being misunderstood. For us, it was a joyful revelation that God made to us. Bit by bit, love began to make headway, more through people's lives than by their words.

The saints were a big help to us from the beginning, especially St. Francis with his cry that "Love is not loved," and St. Catherine with her "Fire of Love."

Years later we see that the Focolare has progressed according to how much it has loved. It has certainly not been scholarly research that advanced the movement in the world. And it has not even been the speeches and talks given, however brilliant they were, unless they *were* charity. Progress has come through the people who loved, often hidden or unnoticed. And with God's grace we have continued to live our ideals, fast learning everything from love, because love is the source of wisdom. We wrote it in our rule, and we made our final end and purpose, "to be perfect in love."

Of one heart and one mind

Everyone agrees that love tends to be mutual, it tends to communion and goes on to a supernatural union, which makes of us one body which is Christ's body.

A consequence of mutual love clear to us in the beginning, as it was also a novelty among the Christians of that time, was that mutual love leads all of us to be of one mind. We were not of one heart only but also of one mind. If we were not of one mind about something, it meant there was disunity, which had to be corrected.

Is this right? Is this Christianity? Is it something to which Christians are bound?

Let's look at how the first Christians lived. St. Paul said to them: "I appeal to you, brethren, by the name of our Lord Jesus Christ, that all of you agree and that there be no dissensions among you, but that you be united in the same mind and the same judgement" (1 Cor 1:10). Among the first Christians the kind of mutual love that led to being of one mind was not just optional advice, but a demand which Paul implored them to fulfill. Having one soul consists in having only one way of thinking, which is Christ's. If we are incorporated into Christ, if we are he, then divisions and diversity in thought signify a divided Christ.

Notice that for Paul unity of thought concerns not only doctrinal points but the whole of life in its Christian practice. When he spoke to the Corinthians he knew that they were not

20

divided on points of doctrine; yet he begged them to have unity of thought in everything.

This ultimate harmony was obtained then, as it is by us now, by a complete sharing of our ideas and inspirations and of our material goods. Anyone who is not poor, at least spiritually, cannot hope to possess the kingdom of God either in oneself or in communion with others.

From the very beginning of the Focolare, it was our unity of mind that always impressed other Christians. I remember that even famous people could not understand how we wanted not only a union of our hearts but also a unity of thought. But they admired still more the evidence that it was really achieved.

Pluralism and unity

We must remember that this is not only the ideal of the early Christians. Paul spoke for every century; therefore, this is the ideal for all Christianity.

We are living in turbulent times when nearly every society is threatened by excessive desire for freedom of thought. It is in the name of free thought that the shadow of doubt is cast upon absolutely everything. In this climate the Church is asking us for unity of thought, at least in the area of doctrine. Paul VI said once in an audience,

> Pluralism then? Yes, a pluralism that takes into account the recommendations made by the Council, provided that it is directed at the *ways* of expressing the truths of faith, not at the content. This is something Pope John XXIII was very clear and direct about: the truths of faith can be expressed in different ways, provided that they all have the same meaning. Pluralism should not give rise to doubts, misunderstandings, or contradictions. It is not meant to legalize subjective opinion in matters of dogma, which would compromise the identity, and therefore the unity of the faith. Progress, yes; enrichment of culture, and encouragement to research; but do not tear down.[1]

In the contemporary situation, which is very different from the world of the first Christians, we see how necessary it is to make our contribution in order to present the genuine, splendid face of the Church to the world.

This can be accomplished through the spreading of a great current of charity. We are aware of the need for a powerful injection of the ideal of charity into all the structures of the Church and into the whole network of Christian life. We must achieve a spiritual communion among Christians or we will never be able to arrive at unity of mind. It seems to us that nothing else could be of such positive usefulness toward achieving material and spiritual progress in the world.

Can you imagine? Through perfect communion and unity, we would permit Christ to live among his own, to take the destiny of humankind into his hands! The pope speaks often about love. The Council underscores it strongly. For us it is a specific vocation, therefore a responsibility.

To lose one's ideas

We know that unity of mind was one of the chief characteristics of the early Christians. But if harmony was threatened, for the sake of oneness of thought it was advised that one should give up his or her own ideas for the sake of preserving unity. Paul wrote to the Romans, "As for the man who is weak in faith, welcome him, but not for disputes over opinions" (Rom 14:1). He did not want any kind of harassment or difference of viewpoint to lead to a breakdown of mutual love. He said on this point:

> If your brother is being injured by what you eat, you are no longer walking in love. . . . Let us then pursue what makes for peace and for mutual upbuilding. . . . It is right not to eat meat or drink wine or do anything that makes your brother stumble. (Rom 14:15, 19, 21)

And when he wrote to the Corinthians it is again clear that he wanted them to give up an idea if necessary to keep their unity intact. He said:

> To have lawsuits at all with one another is defeat for you. Why not rather suffer wrong? Why not rather be defrauded? (1 Cor 6:7)

The damage of which he speaks is also in the sense of giving up and losing one's own point of view.

Endurance was one of the qualities of love that Paul emphasized to maintain mutual charity. But he did not present it as a passive attitude; on the contrary, it was the result of an awareness that to follow Christ and put all of his commands into practice, one must love and embrace the cross. We cannot dispense with it. We are living in illusion if we disregard or discard the cross. Paul begged the Ephesians to live "with all lowliness and meekness, with patience, forbearing one another in love, eager to maintain the unity of the spirit in the bond of peace" (Eph 4:2-3). Patience with one another is a love that knows how to bend and to be flexible rather than to break unity.

We can say that charity has always helped us to know how to bend and not break. There have been moments when a particular course of action seemed the best, yet the Lord suggested to us that for the sake of preserving unity with everybody, it was better to choose the less perfect way, in unity with others. And this pliability has been painful but one of the most useful means to maintain unity in the Focolare.

We are comforted now to see that our ideal* conforms to scriptural descriptions. We felt it in our own hearts, in which charity was the light. Of course it was obscure at times, because it was charity in the midst of difficulties, but still light.

---

* *The word "ideal" is used in the Focolare primarily to mean God, chosen as the one aim in life. Secondly, it also stands for the Focolare's spirituality and the way it is lived in daily life.*

23

The communion of material goods

Let us now consider another aspect of mutual love. To understand it well, we have to keep in mind the way the Acts of the Apostles present the life of the early Christians:

> Now the company of those who believed were of one heart and soul, and no one said that any of the things which he possessed was his own, but they had everything in common. There was not a needy person among them, for as many as were possessors of lands or houses sold them, and brought the proceeds of what was sold and laid it at the apostles' feet; and distribution was made to each as any had need. (Acts 4:32, 34-35)

It is very clear from this description that mutual love leads to the communion of material goods. The same thing happened in the Focolare, both among the Focolarine* and later within the whole community when the members spontaneously gave away their surplus.

In the first community of Jerusalem, communion of goods was not obligatory, but it was still practiced intensely. It seems to me at the present time that the members of the Focolare are acquiring more and more the mentality and the generosity of the early Christians, and though they are under no obligation, they are on the way to achieving a total communion of goods.

Even in the very beginning there were persons who were called to give everything, and there were others who gave as much as they could.

Now we can see that this practice is penetrating among the Volunteers** who deserve to be called "the early Christians of

---

* *Members of focolare centers, small communities of either men or women, whose first aim is to achieve among themselves the unity Jesus prayed for, through their practice of mutual love. Focolarina: a member of a women's focolare center. Plural: Focolarine. Focolarino: a member of a men's focolare center. Plural: Focolarini (also used to indicate men and women collectively).*

** *The Volunteers, who meet in various small groups called nuclei, are internal members of the Focolare movement and promote its goals through living its spirit in the family, at work, in whatever place they occupy in society.*

the twentieth century." Besides offering their economic surplus in the measure their conscience dictates (which also has to consider their relatives and dependents who do not share their ideal) they are beginning to make a sort of inventory of all their possessions, and to put them at the disposal of others who are in need. The fact that they give also part of their own needs to help emerging countries is another confirmation of their intention to conform to the spirit of the early Christians. If the early Christians sold everything they possessed, it was probably because entire families were converted, but this is not generally the case with us. The Volunteers are usually isolated individuals. Their situation and possibilities are therefore totally different; but their good will is the same.

The same thing must be said of the priests who live in communion within the Priests Movement. Naturally there are many priests who live like this outside the Focolare and other similar movements. However, we hope that many more, urged by the Council and by the pope will be able some day to practice the communion of goods so that the Church may become a communion in reality. Only then will it be really poor.

Next let us consider the communion of goods in our youth movement, the new generation, named Gen. One of the strongest points in their "formula" is to have a full communion of all goods. The future will witness how well they can realize it. In any case, this is symptomatic in a world which has to be totally renewed. Next, as we consider the men and women in religious orders, we know that each order has its own way of putting poverty into practice, following the inspiration of its founder. We see a strong trend sweeping through all these orders to live poverty with renewed dedication, following the guidelines of the Council and some under the influence of the Focolare. They too can be considered "early Christians" in the twentieth century.

These signs of genuine Christianity are encouraging, and so we anticipate the future with joy. We must have faith that the return of modern society to the spirit of the early Christians is not a utopian dream. It is essential for accomplishing our goal,

"That they may all be one" (Jn 17:21). The Council says that it can be done:

> He taught us that the new command of love was the basic law of human perfection and hence of the world's transformation. To those, therefore, who believe in divine love, he gives assurance that the way of love lies open to all people and that the effort to establish a universal brotherhood is not a hopeless one.[2]

Poverty

In the passage we read about the communion of goods in the Acts of the Apostles, we note that the early Christians were not detached from their possessions in order to practice poverty as a personal asceticism. Rather, they did it for the sake of unity, so that no one would be in want and that distribution might be made to all according to their needs.

As we compare the way of poverty of the early Christians with our own experience in the Focolare, we can say that for us, too, poverty has meaning only in its contribution towards building unity. Poverty, yes, but for the sake of charity. For us, everything in the Gospels leads to charity.

From the beginning, this was another way in which our movement seemed revolutionary. Most people thought the counsels were means to personal asceticism and perfection. The individualistic concept of Christianity prevailed at that time.

Organized charity

There is more to note from that passage in Acts. The communion of goods was made in an organized way. The proceeds were given to the apostles and were then distributed to each one in proportion to the needs.

I can see that the more we go ahead and the more the headquarters of the Focolare performs its proper functions (the economic one, for example), the closer we are coming to the first

Christians' way of life. We distribute in an organized way all we have among the Focolarini, among the Volunteers, and among the others in the movement. This organization, of course, is planned by human intelligence; but it has as its model the communion of saints. Everything must circulate with wisdom, prudence and generosity.

Equality

Among the early Christians the communion of goods led to equality and it publicly demonstrated that all were brothers and sisters to one another. "But you are not to be called rabbi, for you have one teacher, and you are all brethren" (Mt 23:8).

The call to equality is explicit also in Paul's letters. He always connects it with the communion of goods. He wrote to the Corinthians:

> I do not mean that others should be eased and you burdened, but that as a matter of equality your abundance at the present time should supply their want, so that their abundance may supply your want, that there may be equality. As it is written, "He who gathered much had nothing over, and he who gathered little had no lack." (2 Cor 8:13-15)

Hospitality

The early Christians naturally thought of themselves as merely managers of their own belongings. Evidence of this can be seen clearly from the importance they gave to hospitality. It was practiced certainly because Jesus' own words were fresh in their minds: "When did we see you a stranger and welcome you?" (Mt 25:38); but also because their houses were considered to be the common property of all. Hospitality, too, was a sign of their equality. Since all were equal, all had the same rights. Hospitality is a prominent theme throughout the Bible. For example, Paul urged the Romans: "Share your belongings with your needy brothers, and open your homes to strangers" (Rom 12:13). And Peter said, "Open your homes to each other without complaining" (1 Pt 4:9).

I remember in the beginning how much we tried to practice hospitality. Sometimes there would be a poor person seated next to each Focolarina at the dinner table. It was logical then for us to give up our bed and sleep on the floor when other girls had no shelter. Incidents of this sort sometimes led to the conversion of our guests.

As time went on this spirit of hospitality caught on with the whole community around the focolare center. We still remember how one of the first Focolarini was touched by the way he was received in the house of a member of the community. It was a sure sign of an evangelical life.

Now, in the Focolare, everything is becoming organized. Each person does his or her own job simply because no one person can do everything. And if the focolare center cannot give hospitality to all, there are the Volunteers who want to live the works of mercy. We have the New Families Movement and also we have those priests and religious who have more facilities and often a special vocation to offer hospitality. Throughout the Focolare movement the awareness of the duty of hospitality is constantly increasing.

Humility

The early Christians also put great emphasis on service. "The Son of Man did not come to be served but to serve"(Mt 20:28), and Paul wrote, "Do nothing from selfishness or conceit but in humility count others better than yourselves" (Phil 2:3). Service therefore implies the development of *humility*. In this context I will quote another part of the 1946 notes, where one can clearly see how our Lord was teaching us this virtue along with the other first steps of the ideal. The study of the early Christians now makes me understand how absolutely indispensable it was to stress humility for the new way that we were undertaking.

Charity sums up all virtues. As time went on, we simplified things affirming that charity is our ideal, to the apparent neglect of the other virtues. We did it to characterize ourselves and distinguish better the ideal that God had given us from other ideals of poverty or humility or service. However, at the beginning, since we had received very special gifts of light, we were careful to try to live the other virtues as well. Later on, our rule confirmed this attitude: "Only one thing is necessary: to love God; remember, however, that true love of God is expressed by exercising *all the Christian virtues.*"

But let's go back to humility and the 1946 notes.

> The virtue that unites the soul to God and fuses the human and the divine in the creature is self-annihilation. The tiniest spot of the human which does not let itself be assumed by the divine, breaks unity, with serious consequences. Our unity with God requires total annihilation, the most heroic humility. We must feel at the service of God, always under the loving gaze of a Father, who gives commands in order to accomplish in us his plan, which is our happiness.
>
> Unity is also achieved with others through humility, by constantly aspiring to put oneself as much as possible at the service of one's neighbor. If we want unity, we have only one right: to serve everybody, because in everybody we serve God. As Paul says, "For though I am free from all men, I have made myself a slave to all, that I might win the more" (1 Cor 9:19).
>
> We do not enter into ourselves except to be alone with God and to pray for our neighbors and for ourselves. We should live constantly emptied of self, to be completely in love with the will of God, in love with the will of our neighbor, whom we want to serve for God's sake. A good worker does nothing except what one's employer commands. If all people, or at least a tiny group, were true slaves of God in their neighbor, soon the world would belong to Christ.

It is interesting to note that the word "serve" in the New Testament has two different meanings: sometimes it means "to

29

serve *out of love,*" other times "to serve *like a slave.*" It is well known that slaves in those times had no rights; they existed only for their master. That is how Christians were supposed to look upon everything they had—their work, their own special gifts, their prayers—as a service to their neighbors. For example, on the subject of one's personal gifts Peter wrote, "As each has received a gift, employ it for one another, as good stewards of God's varied grace" (1 Pt 4:10).

On the subject of work, "Let the thief no longer steal, but rather let him labor, doing honest work with his hands, so that he may be able to give to those in need" (Eph 4:28). About prayer, "Epaphras, who is one of yourselves, a servant of Christ Jesus, greets you, always remembering you earnestly in his prayers" (Col 4:12). Prayer as well was put at the service of others. We certainly must revive this sense of humility, and put into practice Luke's words, "Let the greatest among you become as the youngest, and the leader as one who serves" (Lk 22:26). Unfortunately it is not always like this. Overwork sometimes makes the persons in charge assume a high-handed attitude. Our rule states,

> Charity inspiring and shaping the act of giving orders, as the spirit of the Focolare requires, will preserve superiors from an imperious tone, a hateful thing in the eyes of all. Charity instead will make Christian brotherhood radiate with its own characteristic beauty, so that whoever visits the focolare center will always be able to say, "Behold how good and pleasant it is when brothers dwell in unity" (Ps 132:1).

These words express how much it is God's will for us to show pure Christianity in which equality rules, as among the early Christians. We must continue to strive toward this high goal.

The rotten apple

The opposite of mutual love is sin, because we use our neighbors instead of serving them. Paul distinguishes two kinds of sinners, those within the community and those outside of the community. He was very strict with the community. He says that the members should have absolutely nothing to do with one who sins habitually and still calls himself a "brother." He goes as far as to say: "Drive out the wicked person from among you" (Cor 5:13).

For those who failed in various other ways, it is recommended, "Strive for peace with all men, and for the holiness without which no one will see the Lord. See to it that no one fail to obtain the grace of God; that no 'root of bitterness' spring up and cause trouble, and by it many become defiled" (Heb 12:14-15).

Regarding those who did not belong to the Christian community, Paul said not to judge them. This is what we try to practice in the Focolare. In trying to follow the norms of the Gospel we should frankly warn those who make mistakes. And if that gets nowhere, the headquarters of the Focolare should be informed. We must not be surprised if, as a last resort, a person is sent away, with all charity.

The devil knows where to attack. And his methods are really something to fear. It is logical that he would choose to work for him people who have been chosen by God. In any case, the rotten apple must be thrown out, lest it contaminate others. Towards those who do not belong to the Focolare, our hearts should be very open, and we should have the charity which bears all things, believes all things, hopes all things, and also covers all things, in order to open up a possible dialogue with anyone, though always within the limits set by prudence.

Mutual admonition

Mutual admonition, which was very common among the early Christians, is another way to exercise mutual love. Paul wrote: "Teach and admonish one another in all wisdom" (Col 3:16). "Mend your ways, heed my appeal, agree with one another" (Cor 13:2). Also, "Let us consider how to stir up one another to love and good works, not neglecting to meet together, as is the habit of some, but encouraging one another" (Heb 10:24-25).

Correcting and encouraging one another have been essential to us from the start. It was the first thing we did when we met together in the first focolare center. And it kept unity. This aspect of mutual love must be always practiced. We will have to see how mutual admonition as a service to one's neighbor can be applied among all the members of the Focolare.

Mutual correction among the first followers of Jesus shows that a Christian was considered to be part of a family. It is beautiful to see how Paul emphasized helping one another to move ahead, which in practice meant going on to sanctity together. And isn't our idea of "becoming saints together" one of the great novelties for a mass movement? In any case, it is possible to become saints together where there is a collective spirituality. We have tried to attain our personal sanctity through our quest for communitarian sanctity. And that is exactly how the early Christians lived.

Philadelphia

In the early Christian communities, charity, called *philadelphia,* was extended to all. *Philadelphia* literally means *brotherly love.* In classical literature the term was used only for love between blood relatives. It was never used in any other sense, for example, to indicate the members of the same society. The only exception ever to this was in the New Testament.

All this makes us understand this point of our rule better, "The Focolare is a family, united by a supernatural spirit which ought to be greater than the unity of a natural family." It reminds us of an experience at the beginning. One day we had the intuition that we were more of a family to each other than our natural family. We were God's children more than our parents'. For, if we have been incorporated into Christ, it is clear that the reality of this unity must exceed any other. Certainly, the word *philadelphia* testifies that this reality was deeply felt by the early Christians.

Philadelphia as it is described in the New Testament, has all the human characteristics of natural brotherly love, like *strength* and *affection*. Paul says to the Romans: "Love one another with brotherly affection" (Rom 12:10). And Peter wrote, "Above all hold unfailing your love for one another" (1 Pt 4:8). And again: "Love one another earnestly from the heart" (1 Pt 1:22).

It is to be very intense; at the same time, however, it is to be pure. Brotherly love, both strong and tender, should also exist between the ones in authority and the faithful. Paul said, "But we were gentle among you, like a nurse taking care of her children" (1 Thes 2:7). Another consequence of brotherly love is that it excludes *familiarity,* which would make us forget to love Jesus in the neighbor.

People often ask me what my focolare center is like. Basically, the only thing that we always try to have is love which is "naturally supernatural." It is hard to imagine what will happen when one of us dies. Certainly that person will unite heaven and earth and we will feel that we are already in heaven. We will find it hard to believe that we are still standing on this earth, because God has fused us into one soul. This is divine unity that not even God wants to break. Only the failure of our response could do it. One cannot reach this reality in a short time. It is a long, at times hard, way. Most of all, it always demands seeing Jesus in the other person, which is the indispensable condition for overcoming moments of difficulty. In all our focolare centers we feel that, by the grace of God, we are much, much more than a natural family. When one of us visits his or her family, there is a feeling of being "away from home." Our parents cannot regret this since they are glad to have given us to God.

There is going to be more and more need to develop our charity, to refine it, to purify it, to strengthen it, so that love among us becomes as strong as death. That must be its measure. Our greatest help in doing this will be our personal union with God. The deeper our love of God, the more concrete our charity will become towards everyone; and the presence of Jesus in our midst (cf. Mt 18:20) will be evident and capable of changing the world.

THE NAME OF THE MOVEMENT IS CHARITY

Incarnate charity

I often wonder if we know how to express what the Focolare is. Even for me it is not easy to define it. There is a bit of a mystery and it could not be otherwise if it is a Work of God. The Focolare developed through the years, as a whole and in its details, in the image of the Trinity.

St. Cyprian insisted that Christ, in forming his Church, took his inspiration, his model, from the Trinity. "The Lord says 'I and the Father are one.' He regulates the unity of the Church in accordance with the divine unity."[1] And the expression of this saint was inserted at a central point of *Lumen Gentium,* "Thus the Church shines forth as a people made one, with the unity of the Father and the Son and the Holy Spirit."[2] One evening as I went into a church for Mass, I had a sudden intuition that came with tremendous supernatural joy. I understood that our movement could be given a name, the name that Augustine often gave to his Church, that is *charity.*[3] I would call the Focolare charity because everything that is not charity in it ("organized charity" as Pope Paul could call the Church, and "incarnate charity" as the Patriarch Athenagoras would say) is not a living part of it.

As universal as charity

According to our rule, the Focolare has the qualities of charity which we have mentioned. Our movement fosters love for all people, a truly universal love. In fact, our primary, specific purpose is "that they may all be one" (cf. Jn 17:21).

To achieve this purpose, we have initiated mass movements whose future we can only dimly foresee.

By means of the New Families Movement we want to reach the basic cells of society. By means of the New Humanity Movement we want to reach the structures of society. By means of the Parish Movement, we want to reach all the communities which center around a priest. By means of the Priests Movement, we desire to revive charity in the greatest possible number of secular priests. By means of the Movement for Religious, we want to make our contribution to the renewal of religious orders.

Since the Focolare is universal like charity, it has Mary for its model, for she is the mother of all people.

Hope against every hope

From the beginning we always hoped (through the charity that "hopes all things") that some day the Church would allow the Focolare to serve and influence all the vocations of the world. The hope seemed impossible because as far as we know this sort of thing had never been the plan of any movement recently born in the Church. We always struggled for it, knowing how to put aside, for the sake of the authority of the Church, what had been perhaps suggested by wisdom. Now, this wide influence has become God's will for us, as we have it in our rule, approved by the Church.

The "body" of God

Why should the Focolare seek to influence everybody, as charity directs? Because it wants to cooperate with the Council in bringing back the Church and as much as possible all humanity to God's original design.

Recently, I read a study on "Charity in the Second Vatican Council." I was very happy to see that the Holy Spirit in the

Council, in order to give back to the Church its real countenance, demands that it live again in the spirit of the early Christians. For them the original reality of the Church was communion, charity. All the other values in its structure have meaning only in this essential reality.

For this reason Cyprian, though he had great respect for the dignity of the bishop, turned to his clergy and declared, "From the beginning of my episcopate, I have made it a rule not to decide anything without your counsel and the people's consent."[4] Besides the words "common counsel" and "consent," Cyprian used other words, like "co-priests," "co-bishops," "colleagues," all of which express communion. The important common factor for him was this "co-being."

Augustine affirmed: "What consoles me is being with you (in communion, in charity), because I am the bishop *for* you, but I am a Christian *with* you. The former is the name of an office, the latter of a grace."[5]

The fact is that with Christ as its head, the Church really is the "body" of God, and God is charity. Tertullian explained: "Where there are the three, that is, the Father, the Son, the Holy Spirit, there is the Church, which is the body of the three."[6] If this is true, if the Church truly is organized charity, then the Focolare's vocation of proclaiming mutual and constant charity is for all the Church.

The whole Church today and all of us Christians ought to be charity above everything else.

Mercy in action

In another way, the Focolare is charity because it is not limited to the spiritual aspect of charity, but always becomes practical towards our neighbor. This is demonstrated by the vocation of the Volunteers, which consists in the consecration of material things of the world and includes all the works of mercy for the good of humanity. To feed the hungry, to give drink to the thirsty, to clothe the naked (which in the broadest sense means to christianize industry, commerce, and agriculture); to take care of the sick and to console the afflicted (which means to christianize housing, tourism, and transport); to instruct the ignorant (which means to christianize schools and the sciences); to admonish the sinner (which means to christianize the law and the courts) and so on.

The Council says more in this point:

> Light and strength derive from the Christian commitment which helps to establish the community of people according to divine law. Projects are begun for the service of all, but especially for the poor. Not all who say "Lord, Lord" will enter the kingdom of heaven, but those who do the will of the Father by efficaciously setting to work. It is the Father's will that we recognize and really love Christ our neighbor in all people, in word and in action, thereby witnessing to the Truth. This is the way to share with others the mystery of the heavenly Father's love.[7]

Love through the works of mercy is precisely the vocation of our Volunteers. But there is an inherent danger of these works becoming "a clanging cymbal" (cf. I Cor 13:1). This is why we have the focolare centers where charity must be lived in its pure state and radiate in the world. In this lies the great, rare election of the Focolarini who have to consume themselves continually in mutual charity in order to be other Christs.

The Focolare is also charity because it *believes all things.* There are married people who are also Focolarini because of a very special calling, fruit of charity, *which can do all things.* Charity also moves us to *be the first to love.* This is why we approach people who have drifted away from the Church, who have been its enemies at times, and seek to bring them back. Thus our rule tells us to follow Mary and love her as the "refuge of sinners."

The Focolare is charity because it *makes itself one* with the world. And this is what the infinite God did for us: he annihilated himself, became a child and then a grown man, was forsaken and crucified.

The Focolare makes itself one with the world by opening a dialogue with anybody. In this way (since charity can make the deserts bloom), it contributes to restoring natural dignity to every human being, every nationality, every race; it contributes to manifesting all the values and truths that every human being possesses.

Then, as they feel understood, people will desire to know what kind of love carried us to them. They will discover that it does not come from us but from God, and they will recognize the true God through our witness.

The structure of the Church

Paul VI, on his apostolic trip to Asia, met bishops gathered in episcopal conferences, fellow Christians, crowds, workers and young people. But we know of only one case when somebody, using an unexpected but effective expression, said to him that he was "God come down to earth": it was when he lowered his exalted dignity and entered the single room inhabited by a poor sick family in one of the most miserable neighborhoods of Manila. Since its beginning, the Church has been charity and communion. Augustine said that it consists in the "communion of the whole world," and Tertullian said that Christians constitute a "communion of fraternity." But it was characterized also by a rock, Peter, upon whom the entire edifice had to be built, giving rise to its hierarchy.

In the same way, though the Focolare is a fraternity in charity, it has its own structure. But the fact is immediately apparent that even its establishment and hierarchical structure are charity, growing out of charity and demonstrating charity.

And what can we say of charity in the Church? Paul VI in Sydney, when he spoke to the bishops of Australia and the Southern Pacific, said, "The Church is charity, the Church is unity." Just before this he had explained,

38

The first communion (in the Church), the first unity, is that of faith. The second aspect of the Catholic communion is that of charity. You know what supreme importance charity has in the whole of the divine design of the Catholic religion, and what particular place charity has in the connecting fabric of ecclesial unity. We must practice in its ecclesial aspects, which the Council has emphasized, a more conscious and active charity. The people of God must accordingly be progressively educated in mutual love for each of its members; the whole community of the Church must by means of charity feel itself united within itself, undivided, living in solidarity and therefore distinct. Hierarchical relationships, pastoral ones (as is well known), collegial relationships, those between different ministerial functions, social ones, domestic ones all must have running through them an ever active stream of charity, having for its immediate effects service and unity.

This, it seems to us, is the principal virtue demanded of the Catholic Church at this moment of history.[8]

We remember too how Jesus asked a greater charity from St. Peter, before giving him charge of the Church, "Do you love me more than these?" (Jn 21:15), as if to say, "Do you want to serve me directly and in my brothers and sisters more than these others?" The title given to the pope, "Servant of the servants of God," is not an empty phrase, but corresponds to Jesus' original requirement.

The Council adds, regarding the Churches: "The individual young Churches, adorned with the beauty of their own traditions, will have their own place in the ecclesiastical communion, without prejudice to the primary of Peter's See, which presides over the entire assembly of charity."[9] On bishops: "The relationships between the bishop and his diocesan priests should rest above all upon the bonds of supernatural charity."[10] On priests: "All priests are united among themselves in an intimate sacramental brotherhood."[11] And finally on the religious orders: "A well-ordered cooperation is to be encouraged between various religious communities, and between them and the diocesan clergy. This depends especially on a supernatural attitude of hearts and minds, an attitude rooted in and founded upon charity."[12]

The structure of the Focolare

For us, too, since the beginning we have wanted the whole of our structure to be charity. Let us see if love permeates the whole rule. Let us first consider the headquarters of the Focolare. It gathers the whole of the movement into unity. But its guideline is nothing else but love, since the aspects committed to each advisor are an expression of love and are conditioned by the others in unity with the president and the assistant.

In order to function, the Coordinating Council needs perfect mutual understanding. Apostolate depends on economy, on spiritual life, or study, or updating, etc. The same is true for every other aspect of the Focolare. Therefore, in order for the Coordinating Council to perform its functions, the advisors are "forced" by God to love one another and to love each other's responsibilities. The *zones* or geographical areas of the world are represented in the Coordinating Council by their advisors. These entities are offsprings of charity. They are small bodies in themselves, within the whole body of the Focolare and exist only if in unity with the entire movement.

The representatives of the various vocations (single and married Focolarini, Volunteers, Gen, priests, religious, etc.) serve their respective branches and represent them in the Coordinating Council. Though each one is organized and disposed differently, they all fit together in unity, like a rainbow, bright with its different colors.

Let us briefly consider the Focolarini. We can see that every aspect of their everyday lives is love.

What for example is the apostolate, our reaching out to others as Christians? In our rule it is described as principles from the way love acts spontaneously. To make ourselves one, bearing witness wherever we are in society, and even going into dangerous countries are nothing but effects of true charity.

Furthermore, the same could be said of the media we use to spread our life because charity makes us one with our times. Mass media help charity to circulate among all and to create communion. Also it is a means to nourish souls; for another characteristic of charity is that it feeds the life it has produced.

And when we get together this is the impulse and product of charity. For it is love that gathers us together.

"Only one thing is necessary" is written in the rule, when it comes to the spiritual life. And this expression of Jesus brings us back to charity, which here has God for its object and the goal of union with him.

With our health, for example, we see that it is all love, for it is either love for our body to sustain it, or it is crucified love. Sickness, agony (our Mass) and death are expressions of the highest charity as in Jesus forsaken and crucified.

Keeping charity with our environment governs how we dress and the place we live.

Likewise, for our studies, where wisdom is the fruit of charity. The fact that we are in touch with each other around the world is another aspect of charity which makes us one and keeps us united.

Another way we are united is in our economy, for what else is it but the communion of goods?

The same reality can be found if we examine the various aspects of our spirituality as it is described in the rule.

All is charity.

If the two great commandments contain all of the law and the prophets, for us too charity contains *all the rules.*

The guiding principle of all our rules in fact, is Jesus in our midst, and he guarantees the life of charity. Origen says, "When Christ sees two or three gathered together in the faith of His name, He goes there, and is in their midst, drawn by their faith and called forth by their unity of mind."[13]

Let us then always do all we can to attract Jesus into our midst. And along with him, we will be charity, we will be living cells of the Focolare, living members of the post-conciliar Church.

PART II

JESUS IN OUR MIDST

WHERE TWO OR THREE ARE GATHERED IN MY NAME, THERE AM I IN THE MIDST OF THEM

In our Focolare life and rule, we have without a doubt given the foremost place to Jesus in our midst. We know that everything we do is of value if Jesus is in our midst, and nothing is of value if Jesus is not in our midst.

He is, as we wrote, for each member of the movement "the norm of norms, the rule that precedes every other rule."

But as I prepare to speak to you about Jesus in our midst, I sense how arid and cold the juridical expression can be. Jesus in the midst is not just a norm or a rule, though it is true that he does precede every other rule. Jesus in the midst is a person! The most holy and glorious person of Jesus. And it is he that we shall speak about.

When the Focolare first came to life, there was not much talk in Catholic environments about Jesus in the midst of a group of people. The statement of Jesus, "Where two or three are gathered in my name, there am I in the midst of them," which we find in Matthew's Gospel, chapter 18, verse 20, was not particularly emphasized.

Even authoritative people, our superiors, however much they loved us, at one point directed us not to speak of Jesus in the midst. But they retracted these instructions soon afterwards, and we think it was the Holy Spirit who made them do so, leaving us completely free to underline these words of Jesus.

From the very beginning, Jesus in the midst was everything for us—he was life.

And now, after the Council has spoken about this in such an explicit way, it has become a normal thing for many people.

But for my consolation, for the consolation of all of us, I wanted to see if in the early Church they gave this sentence of the Gospel the same importance we (not without—I think—the presence of a charism) find ourselves doing.

In reading the Fathers of the Church, for example, I was astonished to see their line of thought in this regard. Through my contact with them, whom I consider as my fathers, Jesus in the midst took on an even greater universality than I had first sensed within me.

Frequently, in order to explain the nature of God's presence in the Church—and this is of greatest importance, since the Church without Christ in it would be nothing—the Fathers base their explanation on two verses: "Where two or three are gathered in my name, there am I in the midst of them" (Mt 18:20), and "Lo, I am with you always, to the close of the age" (Mt 28:20).

Therefore it is not a question of a mechanical formula to which someone out of habit might have reduced living with Jesus in the midst when seeking to be in agreement with others in this way. No, living with Jesus in our midst, we make ourselves much more vitally a part of the presence of Christ in his Church. And one who is sensitive to the things of God, in living this way, cannot help but feel privileged among others of this world.

Jesus in our midst is God come down among us

We all know that the important choice of the Focolare and of each one of us was the choice of God. In the vanity of all things God shone out as a certainty. We adored him present in the tabernacles, we loved him in our neighbors, we contemplated him beyond the stars in the immensity of the universe.

But one day we were surprised by the thought that such a God who was so close to us with his love, but so far away from us with his majesty, had come down to be near us when we were united, setting his dwelling place among us.

Origen says, "By his power he is near to all. . . . He himself says, 'I am a God near at hand' (Jer 23:23). And he also says, 'Where two or three are gathered in my name, there am I in the midst of them.' "[1]

It is magnificent. And this good fortune has been ours.

Origin links the reality of Jesus in the midst to the characteristic "God who is near" of the Old Testament.

Eusebius of Caesarea, commenting on a passage from Zechariah, writes, "'Sing and rejoice, O daughter Zion! (so it is common in Holy Scripture to call the Church of God on earth, as being as it were a daughter of the heavenly Zion), 'See, I am coming to dwell among you' (Zech 2:14). For we believe," continues Eusebius, "that God the Word dwells in the midst of the Church. As indeed he promised when he said, 'Know that I am with you always, until the end of the world' (Mt 28:20)—and, 'Where two or three are gathered together in my name, there am I in the midst of them.'"[2]

Eusebius also says:

> O Lord, I love and prefer your dwelling place, because you yourself have deigned to live here among men and to set here your dwelling place; for you said: "Where two or three are gathered in my name, there am I in the midst of them."[3]

St. John Chrysostom said:

> Higher than the dignity of the Seraphim is it to stand around the throne of God and to have Him in the midst. But you too, if you wish, can obtain this privilege; God is not just in the midst of the Seraphim, but also in our midst, if we wish so, because it is written, "Where two or three are gathered in my name, there am I in the midst of them."[4]

Jesus in our midst is one form of Jesus' presence

Without our doing a lot of theological or philosophical reasoning, throughout the history of the Focolare we always understood that the presence of Jesus was not limited to his mere physical presence, once in past history and now in heaven. There was the presence of Jesus in the midst of two or more persons, Jesus in the Eucharist, Jesus in his word, Jesus in our neighbor, Jesus in the hierarchy.

Origen, one of the Fathers of the Church who has the most to say about Mt 18:20, says:

> The Gospels realize that he who said in Jesus, "I am the way, the truth, and the life," was not circumscribed, as though the Logos did not exist anywhere outside the soul and body of Jesus. . . . Jesus himself also raises the thoughts of those learning from him to greater conceptions of the Son of God when he says: "Where two or three are gathered together in my name, there am I in the midst of them."[5]

He also says:

> Do not be afraid, even though [Jesus] has been taken up now into heaven, he will return. . . . I repeat, do not be afraid; Jesus Christ is being sent to us right now. It is not a lie. . . . "Where two or three are gathered in my name, there am I in the midst of them."[6]

St. Cyril of Alexandria says:

> All those who think rightly and have solid faith must convince themselves that, though he is far from us with his body, that is, though he has returned to God the Father, nonetheless he governs the world with his divine power and authority and he is present in the midst of those who love him.
> Thus he said, "Truly I say to you . . . where two or three are gathered in my name, there am I in the midst of them."[7]

Jesus in the midst is immediately present

We establish the presence of Jesus in the midst whenever we want it. We can live it immediately. Origen says that one should "not let this also pass unobserved, that he did not say, 'Where two or three are gathered in my name, there *will* I be in the midst of them,' but, 'there *am* I.' "[8]

Also Theophylact, Bishop of Bulgaria, says: "He doesn't say 'I *will* be', as if putting off or delaying his presence, but 'I *am*,' that is, I am already there."[9]

Jesus in the midst is the Church

We have always liked the saying of Tertullian: "Where three [are gathered together], even if they are laymen, there is the Church."[10]

Yes, because we are often a small group united and juridically grafted onto the entire Church of Christ; therefore, even if there are few of us, we are Church, living Church, through the presence of Jesus among us.

John of Cyparission confirms it:

> The Church of God . . . is the sacred assembly in the name of the true light that enlightens every man who comes into the world, an assembly which rises and grows not only from multitudes or fortunate men, but also from those who are humble. There is a passage where the Word of God said: "Where two or three are gathered in my name, there am I in the midst of them."[11]

Jesus in our midst brings churches to birth

And since we are Church, we are capable of generating churches. This is what happens with missionaries who go to some far-off place that has not yet been evangelized and found a church, the local church.

This is what happened with us, too, in Fontem (West Cameroons), for example, where the first two or three Focolarini, though they were laymen, succeeded in building up a parish which is an integral part of the diocese of Buea, because Christ was among them.

Eusebius of Caesarea used the phrase "city of God" to describe the universal Church and "houses of this city" for the local Christian communities, to which he often applies Mt 18:20. He says:

> The churches, later established all over the world, are those houses in whose midst God is always present. He who said, "Where two or three are gathered in my name there am I in the midst of them."[12]

Elsewhere he affirms:

> These idolatrous forms ceased to be when churches were founded throughout Egypt and the Lord went there and visited his churches, as he said, "Where two or three are gathered in my name, there am I in the midst of them."[13]

Jesus in the midst is salvation in difficulties

Jesus in the midst is the salvation of the Movement and the very possibility of its life in regions where external conditions hinder its free development, either because of other religions which are intolerant towards ours, or because the environment has become dechristianized by a materialistic mentality and way of life, or because of the complete absence—as in non-Christian countries—of any knowledge of Jesus. In areas as such our homes are our meeting places and Jesus in the midst makes them into churches.

Circumstances of this kind bring us back to the situation of the early Church.

In the *Apostolic Constitutions*, which is the most important juridical-liturgical collection of early Christianity, we find written:

> If it be not possible to assemble either in the church or in a house, let everyone by himself sing and read and pray, or two or three together. For, "Where two or three are gathered together in my name, there am I in the midst of them."[14]

Tertullian in *De fuga in persecutione* writes: "Are you unable to go to all the meetings? Then for you, even if you are only three, let that be the Church."[15]

Theodore the Studite says:

> Brothers and Fathers, God has granted us a supreme favor, that of being persecuted for his sake, as the Gospel says: "Blessed are those who are persecuted for righteousness' sake, for theirs is the kingdom of heaven" (Mt 5:10).
>
> But we must take care that it is not for living a life unworthy of beatitude—a life not lived according to the Gospel—that we receive persecution as a punishment.
>
> Therefore, one who is persecuted must, first of all, not live alone, but live together with another brother, because, "Where two or three are gathered in my name, there am I in the midst of them," says the Lord.[16]

For Theodore, Jesus in the midst guarantees the authenticity of a life lived according to the Gospel.

Jesus in our midst unites us even over distance

St. Athanasius applies Mt 18:20 also to those who are far from one another, yet spiritually united. This is of great joy to us.

> Although distance divides us, nonetheless . . . the Lord . . . unites us spiritually in harmony and in the bond of peace.
>
> When we have these sentiments and raise the same prayers [to God] no distance can separate us, because the Lord unites us and binds us closely together. For where two or three are gathered together in his name, he himself is present in the midst of them as he promised.[17]

Jesus in our midst and unity with the whole Church

There is a mysterious and marvelous fact in our Focolare lives. Who was it who always convinced us, beyond the slightest

51

doubt, that everything we did was of value if it was done in unity with the Church, the hierarchically constituted Church? Who was it who impressed in our hearts the conviction that the Church has always been a mother to us, even when someone not too well-versed in the works of God might have doubted it, and that as a consequence our lives had to be lived as children of this mother? What was it that gave such importance to Jesus in our midst, whom we tried to have present in all our gatherings, if not the faith and conviction that he was there in our midst because our little group was united to the great Church and to its shepherds?

Thinking back at it now, and thinking of our age at that time, it is enough to make us dizzy. We could have gone astray on this point a thousand times, but we never did. This leaves us to say that the one who guided us along the way must have been the Holy Spirit.

On this point, too, the Fathers strongly confirm the line we held to.

St. Cyprian says:

> Nor let certain people deceive themselves by a foolish interpretation of the Lord's words: "Wherever two or three are gathered together in my name, I am with them." . . . He teaches us that we must at all times be closely united with one another. But what sort of agreement will a man make with another if he is out of agreement with the body of the Church itself and with the brethren as a whole? How can two or three gather together in Christ's name, if they have obviously cut themselves off from Christ and his Gospel? For it is not we who have left them, but they who have left us, and by setting up conventicles in opposition and thus creating new sects and schisms, they have cut themselves off from the source and origin of [the Christian] realities.
>
> No, the Lord is speaking of his Church; he is telling those who are in the Church, that if they are of one mind, if, as he commanded and taught, even two or three gather and pray in unison, they shall, though but two or three, obtain from God's majesty what they ask for. . . . Therefore, when he lays down in his

commands: "Wherever two or three shall be, I am with them," he does not mean to separate men from the Church which he founded and built himself.[18]

Jesus in our midst: brother, master, guide, strength, light; we have no cause to envy those who lived with him in Palestine. We can hope for everything from this tremendous promise. He is the source of a divine blaze of fire wherever he is in the world: "I came to cast fire upon the earth" (Lk 12:49).

We have a huge treasure, we have *the* treasure; let us leave behind everything in order to possess it; he will give us heaven on earth and in the next life as well.

THE VALUE OF JESUS IN OUR MIDST

Being alone and being united

Let us now say something about being alone and being united.

I remember that especially in the beginning when we first started to live this spirit each one of us felt a strong difference between being united, and being alone without the help of unity.

When we were alone, separated from the community, we became aware of all our personal fragility, we experienced great confusion, our will was weak and unable to carry things through. We could no longer see why we had left everything to follow Jesus. The light was missing; yes, the light.

I remember one day I was alone in the first Focolare house. I was preparing dinner. Through someone's lack of virtue before each of us had left for work, we did not part in full unity. I found I couldn't understand anything anymore. I couldn't see the reason for the many sacrifices I had made to follow Jesus, such as leaving my family whom I loved so much. I couldn't see the reason why I had abandoned so many things for him, like my studies for example. At one point during the day I was up in the attic getting wood for the fire, and I caught sight of the boxes which contained the books I had loved so much. I remember the tears that fell onto the dust that now covered that previous love of mine. And I decided to wait for my friends' return so that we could put Jesus back in our midst. And that's precisely what happened.

When we were united, on the other hand, we felt all the strength of Jesus among us. It was as if we were all clothed in the power and blessing of heaven. We felt capable of the noblest actions for God, the most ardent, difficult resolves, which we subsequently maintained; whereas before, when alone, for all our good will, it was difficult to fully live up to the promises we had made to the Lord. We felt a power that was not merely human.

One of the things that young people have to overcome, for example, is human respect—worrying about what other people think. In unity, this problem no longer existed, not through anyone's personal virtue but through the strength of unity. We spoke instead of "divine respect," that is, our duty of respecting and witnessing to the things of God.

If, before this new life began, we were convinced that it was impossible to live the Gospel in our times because by ourselves we had no success in doing so, afterwards in unity we saw it was possible. It was a huge discovery, rich in consequences, which caused the birth of this vast movement.

The Fathers of the Church use magnificent words to praise being together and to warn against being alone.

Gregory of Agrigentum says:

> Besides, even if we happen to find someone who is all alone, whom we know to be a good and humane person, better than someone else who is not so humane ... nonetheless wise Ecclesiastes' standpoint is to view honest, like-minded men two by two, refuting any kind of objection to such an approach by saying, "For if they fall, one will lift up his fellow" (Eccl 4:10).
>
> If someone falls into that which is forbidden and nowhere finds another person to lift him up and call him back to a better life, it is clear that his fall and his aberration in sin will remain and that he will continue on unchanged or uncorrected.
>
> For this reason, our Lord says in the Gospel: "Where two or three are gathered in my name, there am I in the midst of them," thus clearly teaching us the greater importance and worth of the concord and harmony of two or three in doing good than the goodness of one alone.[1]

Niceta Pectoratus writes:

> Gathering together in one house is safer than being alone. The holy words of our Lord Jesus, in fact, attest to the necessity

of meeting together; for, "Where two or three are gathered in my name, there am I in the midst of them."

Concerning the danger of solitude, Solomon says: "Woe to him who is alone when he falls and has not another to lift him up" (Eccl 4:10b) . . . And regarding the disciples of the Lord it is said: "Now the company of those who believed were of one heart and one soul" (Acts 4:32) . . .

It is therefore necessary that we live together in unity, whereas solitude is unsafe and dangerous.[2]

In his commentary on Psalm 133 ("Behold how good and pleasant it is when brothers dwell in unity! . . . for there the Lord has commanded the blessing") John Chrysostom explains:

"There"—where? Wherever there is such a dwelling place, such harmony, such accord, such living together. Because this implies a blessing, just as its opposite implies a curse.

For this reason someone has praised this with the words . . . "A brother helped is like a strong city" (Prov 18:19).[3]

Elsewhere still, John Chrysostom affirms splendidly that "great is the strength which comes from being together . . . because, when we are gathered together, charity grows, and if charity grows, there is necessarily a growth [among us] of the reality of God."[4]

This Father gives us as an example the unity between Peter and John. In his comment on the verse of the Acts of the Apostles: "Now Peter and John were going up to the temple at the hour of prayer, the ninth hour" (Acts 3:1), he writes:

Do not through negligence let this account pass unobserved, but right from the start try to understand what great charity they had, what great harmony and accord, and how they shared everything and did all things bound by the tie of friendship in God, and how they appeared together at table, when praying, when walking, and in every other action.

Because, if they who were the pillars and the towers [of the Church] and had great trust in God, needed mutual aid and corrected one another, how much more in need of mutual aid are we, weak, wretched, worthless men? . . .

Thus were Peter and John, and they had Jesus in the midst (*habebant Jesum in medio*). "Where two or three are gathered in my name," he [Jesus] says, in fact, "there am I in the midst of them."

Do you understand the importance of being united?[5]

Conditions for having Jesus in our midst

But what conditions are needed for having Jesus in our midst?

We know the answer: we have Jesus in our midst if we are united in his name. This means if we are united in him, in his will, in love which is his will, in mutual love which is the supreme will of Jesus, his commandment, where there is unity of heart, of will, and of thought, if possible in all things, but certainly in matters of faith.

The Fathers of the Church also ask themselves what conditions are required for having Jesus in the midst and from their texts we can infer that one of them sees the same reality from one point of view, and another sees it from another point of view, and so on.

Basil asks: "In what way can we become worthy of having Jesus in the midst of ourselves united in his name?" And he makes living according to the will of God the essential condition.

He says:

> Those who meet together in the name of someone else have to know well the will of the person who has gathered them together, and have to conform themselves to that will. . . .
>
> And so we [monks], who have been called by the Lord, have to recall what the Apostle [Paul] said: "[I] beg you to lead a life worthy of the calling to which you have been called, with all lowliness and meekness, with patience, forebearing one another in love, eager to maintain the unity of the spirit in the bond of peace. There is one body and one spirit" (Eph 4:1- 4).[6]

For Basil, therefore, doing the will of God is the condition required for having Jesus in the midst.

John Chrysostom makes the condition for having Jesus in the midst that of loving our neighbors out of love for Jesus, and loving them as Jesus did, who gave his life for his enemies.

He explains the verse "Where two or three are gathered in my name, there am I in the midst of them," by saying:

> What then? Can we not find two or three gathered together in his name? Yes, but rarely so. In fact [Jesus] is speaking of something more than a mere meeting together. . . . His words have this meaning: If anyone holds me as the principal motive of his love towards his neighbor, then I will be with him. . . . Nowadays, instead, we see that the great majority of people have other motives for their friendship. One loves because he is loved, another loves because someone has been useful to him in some worldly affair; others love for other analogous reasons. But it is difficult to find someone who sincerely loves his neighbor for Christ, as he ought to love him. . . . When someone loves in this manner (that is, for Christ) even if he is hated, insulted, or if his life is even threatened, he goes on loving. . . . For Christ loved his enemies in this way . . . with the greatest love.[7]

For Chrysostom, therefore, loving in the way that Jesus loved is the condition for having Jesus in the midst.

Theodore the Studite finds mutual love to be the condition for having Jesus in the midst of two or more persons. He writes:

> Therefore I heartily beg you in the Lord, not just to look out for your own security in life, but to take care of your brothers, so that you may also be loved by them and that again you may love them in return, for in this way you will love and also be loved.
>
> In fact, where there is spiritual charity, there Christ is in the midst, as he promised.[8]

Origen holds that the condition for having Jesus in the midst is "accord" between several people in thought and in sentiment, so as to arrive—as he says magnificently—at that concord which "unites, and contains the Son of God."[9] He also affirms:

> When Christ sees two or three gathered together in the faith of his name, he goes thither, and is in their midst, drawn by their faith and called by the unity of their mind.[10]

To his mind there are never more than a few who are united in such a way as to have Christ present, and among the examples he gives he mentions Peter, James and John, "to whom, because they were in unison with one another, the Word of God manifested his own glory." And Paul and Sosthenes "were in unison . . . when writing the first Epistle to the Corinthians; after this Paul and Timothy when sending the second Epistle to the same. And even three were in unison when Paul, Silvanus and Timothy gave instruction by letter to the Thessalonians."[11]

But he also mentions the early Christians who were of one heart and one mind (Acts 4:32), adding however, "if it is possible for such a condition to be found among many."[12]

After these considerations it is clear how precious is the vocation of our movement. In the Focolare this life is extended to many, a life that some Fathers of the Church maintained belonged to only a few, whereas the others saw it as the vocation of the entire Church. We are therefore grateful to God and with all our soul we cling to this calling which is still so rare in the world today.

The value of Jesus in our midst

But what is the value of Jesus in our midst?

In the early years of the Focolare, when the prevailing characteristic was the ardor of "beginners," in a warm, filial talk that I had with the then Monsignor Montini, we spoke about the way we Christians often fall into misplacing values when we consider the various riches of the Church.

That brief conversation had to do precisely with the value of Jesus in the midst, and the ideas touched on during it were something of the following:

If we are united, Jesus is among us. This is something precious—more precious than any other treasure that our hearts may possess: more than mother, father, brothers and sisters, children. It is worth more than our house, our work, or our belongings; more than the works of art in a great city like Rome; Jesus in the midst is worth more than magnificent monuments, more than luxurious mausoleums, more than the splendor of the Vatican: more than our own souls!

Just recently, I was particularly happy to come across a statement of Gregory Nazianzen, which bears some similarity to that conversation. In his famous farewell address in Constantinople, delivered before the public among whom there were also various bishops, he says: "But you [Constantinople] had such an ardent love for frescoes, paintings, tombstones carved with art and elegance, long arcades and galleries, and you shined all ablaze with gold . . . certainly not knowing that . . . three who are gathered together in the name of the Lord are deemed by God more numerous than many thousands who deny his divinity [that is, more than your entire population]."[13]

I also recall, regarding the value of Jesus in the midst, the brief words which Father Foresi* said during his first trip to the United States, to the few Focolarini there during the final Mass.

He said that he had seen many beautiful things in New York City, but that the most beautiful of all for him was that tiny group of Focolarini who had Jesus in their midst.

Jesus in our midst is a light

Jesus in the midst is a light.

At the *Genfest*** the Holy Father told us something that is good to remember when he invited us to follow two sentences of the Gospel. One of these is: "You have one teacher" (cf. Mt 23:8, 10).

---

* *Pasquale Foresi is the first Focolarino to be ordained a priest. He is considered by Chiara Lubich, together with Igino Giordani, to be a co-founder of the Focolare.*

** *Focolare youth festival held in Rome on March 1 and 2, 1975 with 25,000 participants.*

With this the Holy Father stressed the line of action that has been ours since the start.

Who so enlightened us regarding the phrases of the Gospel that we were able to see it as something completely new, revolutionary, and full of life? Jesus in our midst.

Origen says that Jesus, present among people who are united in his name, "is ready by his presence with power to illumine the hearts of those who truly desire to become his disciples."[14] With these words he leads us to understand that he is not speaking of just an intellectual enlightenment, but of a vital and sapiential illumination which extends to the whole person.

And who, then, throughout the entire history of the Focolare, traced those lines of light for the organization of the movement?

Who else gave birth to the various vocations, if not he? Each vocation is divine and so, too, is the way the same ideal is applied to the various callings.

He is the one behind our norms of life, behind every step we take.

And when the course of action to take is unclear, to whom else do we turn but to him, saying among ourselves: "Come, let's put Jesus in our midst so we can understand the will of God?"

He alone is the light to our life, the answer to our every problem.

Origen, too, realized this when he wrote:

> If there is an uncertainty which we are unable to resolve or find a solution for, let us go, united in heart in regards to the question at hand to Jesus, who is present where two or three are gathered together in his name, and is ready by his presence with power to illumine the hearts of those who truly desire to become his disciples.[15]

Jesus in the midst is festivity

When Jesus is in our midst there is always a festive atmosphere.

If there is one thing characteristic of our meetings, both small and large, it is the fullness of joy that radiates from each person, that lights up each face.

It often happens that when you take part in one of these meetings you find yourself asking if it isn't a holiday.

Vice-versa, it happens that on some Sundays when you find yourself all alone, without your companions, you feel that the day of the Lord has lost its splendor.

Yes, because Jesus in the midst of a small group or a large number gathered together in his name is the Jesus of "the feast," Jesus of the resurrection, who now, besides living at the right hand of the Father, also lives in the little churches made up of several Christians.

John Chrysostom says:

> Even though Pentecost day is over, the feast is not at an end; whenever we assemble there is festivity. From what do we deduce this? From the very words of Christ who says: "Where two or three are gathered in my name, there am I in the midst of them." Therefore, each time that Christ is present in the midst of a gathering, what greater proof could you ask than that it is a festive occasion?[16]

When Jesus is in our midst it is a time of festivity for us, and also for him.

Theophylact, Bishop of Bulgaria, confirms it: "Truly God rejoices not in a great crowd, but rather 'where two or three are gathered in his name, there he is in the midst of them.' "[17]

If God rejoices where there is unity, what ideal could be greater than to make one's life a succession of days that add additional joy to the happiness that Jesus already experiences?

His love for us, his measureless love of every day, that reaches us in big things and in the tiniest ones, calls for and deserves it.

A COMMUNITY WHICH HAS JESUS IN ITS MIDST

Jesus in the midst and community life

Christianity in its various manifestations, as we know, is always new and always the same. If we ask ourselves, in a nutshell, what a focolare center is, we can and should define it as follows: it is a little community which has Jesus in its midst.

When God thought of founding monasteries, for example, his idea then was the same.

Indeed, what other idea could God have, after sending his Son for the salvation of the human race, if not that of wanting to continue in some way his presence among the lives of human beings.

We find in the writings of Theodore Balsamon:

> Therefore we say that since the mouth of God has declared, "where two or three are gathered in my name, there am I in the midst of them" (Mt 18:20), it is necessary that there be at least three to found anything that can be called a monastery.[1]

A monastery, therefore, is a real monastery if it has the presence of Jesus among at least three members.

Of course, while Christianity is always the same—and this is to the praise of God's Unity—still there are no two cases completely alike, just as there are no two leaves of a tree totally identical—and this is to the praise of God's Trinity.

A focolare center is not the same thing as a monastery.

The Focolare with Jesus in the midst has norms that we believe to be inspired, and that have been blessed and approved by the Church.

The focolare center is a house in which life is ordered according to the various aspects we are all familiar with. These range from a complete communion of goods to a specific apostolate, to set prayers, to levels of formation for its members who have left the world for God and consecrated themselves with vows, to a determinate way of viewing one's physical health, to a particular way of laying out the various rooms of the house, to studies both religious and secular, to unity among all the members spread all over the world, unity maintained via all the means available.

These are the elements which shape and in their turn facilitate the presence of Jesus in our midst.

What, on the other hand, is the definition of a monastery?

John, Bishop of Antioch (twelfth century), tells us:

> Do you not know what a monastery is? It is a house that is wholly sacred, built in the name of Christ our God, in whose holy, innermost rooms there are paintings of him, of his astonishing and divine sufferings. In its church are the sacred books and the precious vestments and vessels.
>
> In the monastery is the holy community of those who for God have renounced the world, everything in the world, and their very selves. They are with God, they listen to him day and night, they sing and recite psalms. . . . And they have him always in their midst, according to the most certain promise of God: "Where two or three are gathered in my name there am I in the midst of them."[2]

Basil, in his rule for the monks of the Eastern Church, identifies monastic life with being gathered together in the name of Jesus.

The value that he gives to a life in common probably springs from his personal experience. Gregory the Presbyter wrote that St. Basil and St. Gregory Nazianzen, as they were

> educated together in cultural studies and separated from one another for a short time, hurried to be near one another again. . . so that in them these words were fulfilled: "Where two or three

are gathered in my name, there am I in the midst of them." Moreover, while remaining together, they not only grew in virtue by being a source of encouragement for one another, but they also composed the laws of monastic life for religious men consecrated to God and detached from the world.[3]

As I set out to deepen my knowledge of the presence of Jesus in our midst, I understand more and more its immense wealth and divine reality. When two of us in the Focolare are united, let us remember that we are not two, but three. When we are three, we are four. . . . We must open up the eyes of our souls to see Jesus always there with us, taking part in our studies, our work, our sufferings, and our joys.

We must pay attention in our lives not to lose any of the value or the effects that his presence implies.

At times, for example, we might be led to consider the presence of Jesus in the midst a mere instrument for the apostolate of the Focolare, since we know how extraordinarily effective it is, and we could live on without seeing the Focolare as a jewel in and of itself. And don't we feel ours the words of St. Basil when he says "we should perform every action as if under the eyes of the Lord, and think every thought as if observed by him"?[4]

Again, the Focolarini have certain practices of piety established by their rule which they perform individually (owing to the type of life that characterizes the focolare center) wherever the will of God places them. Only in the Centers of the Movement where Focolarini, besides living under the same roof, also work together, are we invited to perform these practices in common.

Here, too, Basil's ideas can be helpful to the Focolarini:

If some, perhaps, are not in attendance because the nature or place of their work keeps them at too great a distance, they are strictly obliged to carry out, wherever they are, with promptitude, all that is prescribed for common observance, for "where two or three are gathered in my name," says the Lord, "there am I in the midst of them."[5]

Therefore, when we pray, we must realize we are united to the chorus of prayers that all the Focolarini of the world send up to God, and we must be convinced of this further assertion of Basil's:

> Even prayer itself which does not come from persons praying together is much feebler, the Lord having declared that he will be in the midst of two or three who call upon him with oneness of mind.[6]

Basil speaks of Jesus in the midst again at various points in his rule. One part which I feel to be especially interesting for us is this magnificent passage on poverty and God's providence.

The Focolarini too have placed all their goods in common, "down to the pin" as we say, and they too are daily witnesses to the providence of God, which is usually never lacking if we live the spirit of Christ. And it is this phenomenon which amazes us and shows us the truth of Jesus' promise to give the hundredfold in brothers, sisters, mothers, and goods to those who leave all things to follow him (cf. Mt 19:29; Mk 10:30).

Now according to Basil:

> It is proper that once an ascetic has taken up that life in common which we have spoken about, he be free of every personal possession of earthly goods.
>
> Because if he is not thus free, in the first place with his private property he ruins a perfect and pure fellowship, and in the second place he reveals himself to be without faith, as if he had no confidence that God will nourish those who are united in his name. . . .
>
> For, if where two or three are gathered together in the name of Christ he is in the midst of them, there is all the more reason why he will be present where there is a constant meeting of a much larger number of people.
>
> Therefore, either we will have everything we need as long as Christ is present among us, just as the Israelites in the desert had everything which could be useful to them, or else, even if we are lacking in something in order that we might be tested, it is better

that we be in need and be with Christ rather than possess all the wealth of the world and not be united with him.[7]

What we have said here about the focolare centers holds as well for those other forms of living in unity present in the movement, which we might call temporary focolare units, such as the nuclei of Volunteers, of priests, of men and women religious, the Gen units, and so on, provided that they too remain all day long in unity of spirit with the other members of the nucleus, the unit, and the other members of the entire Work of Mary, so as to always have the presence of Jesus in their midst.

And what we have said here about the focolare centers also holds for those compound forms of community life, where we find present together focolare centers, nuclei, units, new families, and new communities of religious . . . that is to say, our little cities which reproduce today in a modern form those communities which once arose around Benedictine monasteries and which were true little cities.

I think we can wish our little cities, though in the midst of inevitable human limitations, that same wish that Theodore the Studite wrote to a monastery that had Jesus in the midst:

> What else is left to say? Just as the grace of our Lord Jesus Christ has brought you together and bound you in spiritual accord, and marked you out by your unanimous agreement, making you shine out in these places like unwavering stars shine in the dark night of heresy; so remain this way in the future, just as you are, unanimous, with the same sentiments, the same thoughts . . . luminous and bright and radiant, and full of wisdom as well, so that you too may be worthy of the words of the Lord: "You are the light of the world" (Mt 5:14), and also "You are the salt of the earth" (Mt 5:13).
>
> And perhaps also, because you live in hilly terrain, it is right that people sing of you: "A city set on a hill cannot be hid" (Mt 5:14)—certainly it is the hilltop of your sublime common life— those who have climbed it live there on earth as it is in heaven (cf. Mt 6:10); the world is not worthy of them, as the Apostle said (cf. Jn 17:16).[8]

Praying with Jesus in our midst—the "consenserint"

There is a prayer which for thirty years, since the Focolare began, has been used by its members. If you ask them to pray in any kind of circumstance, for the living or for the dead, or to obtain any grace at all, they—as we know—make a *consenserint,* that is, united in the name of Jesus, they ask the eternal Father anything whatsoever. And the term *consenserint* is taken from Jesus' statement:

> Again I say to you, if two or three agree (*consenserint*) on earth about anything they ask, it will be done for them by my Father in heaven. For where two or three are gathered together in my name, there am I in the midst of them. (Mt 18:19-20)

Certainly we do not overlook the other prayers that the Church recommends, but this prayer, I would say, is our special one. In this prayer we know that we are not the ones who ask, but Jesus present in our unity. Through this prayer countless graces, spiritual and material, have been showered on the movement.

John Chrysostom says that no one meets together with others to pray

> trusting in his own virtue, but rather in the multitude, in agreement, which God holds in the highest consideration and by which he is moved and appeased.
>
> For, "where two or three are gathered in my name," Jesus says, "there am I in the midst of them." ... What a person cannot obtain praying on his own, he will obtain praying together with many. Why? Because although there is not great strength in personal virtue, there is in unanimity—"where two or three are gathered."[9]

Furthermore, what has always been recognized within the Focolare as a light giving great hope, a light with a truly evangelical dimension, is that "anything" that Jesus says to ask for. Anything, therefore, everything, from little things to big ones, from things for our bodies to things for our spirits. Everything can be asked for in unity. And everything has been asked for in unity.

Peter Chrysologus, in one of his sermons, confirms this:

> The verse states that "if two of you shall agree on earth about anything at all for which they ask, it shall be done for them.". . . Christ did not mention one thing or another, but he promised to do everything—whatever the united request desires.[10]

In our movement, we have not neglected personal prayer. The way of sanctity which our spirituality sets us on, through the various steps which lead along this way, also deepens our personal union with God, which leads us to ask many things of the Lord.

But we are in full agreement with what Peter Chrysologus says:

> Christ promises that he will be in the midst of two or three who are gathered, and that he will give everything they request of him. If this is so, where are those who presume that the congregation of the Church can be disregarded, and assert that private prayers should be preferred to those of an honorable assembly?[11]

Therefore God desires not individualism but rather unity.

Of course, we always thought that the above-mentioned statement of the Gospel obtains its end if lived along with all the rest of the Gospel. For this reason, before making a *consenserint,* we examine ourselves to see if we are ready to die for one another, and we do not slacken this readiness after having prayed. For us, the *consenserint* is the prayer of those who live the Gospel, and not a magical formula for those who need to obtain something.

John Chrysostom explains well the reasons for which we sometimes do not obtain what we have asked for.

> Is there any place where two persons are of one accord? Yes, in many places, or rather, surely everywhere. Why then, you may object, do they not obtain everything they ask for? There are

many reasons which prevent their receiving what they requested. Often they ask things that are not useful or fitting. . . . Others are unworthy and do not do their part. . . . Jesus seeks people who are similar to the apostles. For this reason he says, "If two *of you* agree . . . ," that is, of you who practice the virtues and who live a life according to the Gospel.

Still others pray against those who have offended them, calling down punishment and vengeance, and this kind of thing has been forbidden by a clear commandment: "Pray for those who persecute you" (Mt 5:44).

Some, finally, ask God for mercy, but without repenting of their sins. . . .

But if there are all the conditions called for, that is, if you ask fitting things, if you do all your part, if you live a life like that of the apostles, if you have unity of thought with your neighbor and love for him, you will obtain what you ask for. For the Lord is good and merciful.[12]

We have observed that the *consenserint* bears a great advantage—it prevents our becoming proud, which is almost inevitable in us poor humans, when we get what we have asked for. This is so because we know that with the *consenserint* not only is it Christ in our midst who is asking, but also that we are joined with others in asking.

Listen to how well Anastasius of Sinai explains this idea:

The Lord, who knows well the various thoughts and the pride of man, wants us not to have trust in ourselves, no matter how much we may lead a life dedicated to virtue and sanctity, but rather that, when we ask something, we hold ourselves to be unworthy of obtaining what we wish for, and therefore we unite ourselves to others who think and feel as we do.

One who prays and obtains on his own often becomes proud; whereas we remain within the limits of humility if there are more than one to pray and obtain.[13]

The focolare centers; the other forms of life in the movement; the little cities which echo in this twentieth century the historical forms of religious life which through the course of time have added splendor to the Church; and the *consenserint*, a prayer which is infallible if there are all the required conditions—these are the points we wanted to underline here.

May God make us more and more worthy of such a high vocation, and may he fill our hands with graces to give others in a world that is cold and arid and that doesn't know what it means to live in relationship with a Father who would like, once again, to give to all people the presence of his own Son, and along with him, many, many graces.

JESUS IN THE MIDST AND THE LIFE
OF THE CHURCH

In the three preceding conversations, it was almost as if we wanted to consult the Fathers of the Church, out of respect for their authority, to find support and encouragement concerning the way that God has led us to understand his words: "Where two or three are gathered in my name, there am I in the midst of them" (Mt 18:20).

The Fathers, I think, have answered generously.

Jesus in the midst and the saints

The question that now comes to mind is this: Was it only the Fathers who spoke so explicitly of Jesus in the midst?

We could trace this theme in depth through the entire history of the Church. We can say, however, that when reading the lives of the saints, for example, we often found these words of Jesus emphasized and under different kinds of circumstances. I have also experienced this in recent months.

St. Bede the Venerable, who is also a Father of the Church, was so penetrated by these words that they came to mind as he commented on the following passage of Luke's Gospel: "As they were saying this, Jesus himself stood among them, and said to them, 'Peace to you . . . why are you troubled . . . it is I' " (Lk 24:36, 38, 39). Bede says:

> The first thing in this passage to note and to bear carefully in mind is that God deigned to be present in the midst of the

72

disciples who were speaking about him, and to reveal his presence, letting them see him. This is the same thing that he had promised in another text to all his disciples: "Where two or three are gathered in my name, there am I in the midst of them." Indeed, in order to confirm our faith, he wanted now and then to appear in bodily form as well, thus making visible what he is always doing through the presence of his divine love. Although we may be much less than the apostles, we must believe that through his mercy the same thing happens for us, too. That is, he is in the midst of us each time we meet together in his name.[1]

Sometimes we wonder, when we consider the great light that we feel has overwhelmed us in these past thirty years, what testament we would like to leave behind for those who follow in our path. And, without a doubt, our choice would be the very same testament that Jesus left—mutual love, unity, which brings the presence of Jesus in the midst.

Only by leaving this presence of Jesus in every corner of the world where the Focolare lives, can we be certain that everything will continue to grow, and that he will continue to be teacher, guide, father, and leader of each group of people, small or large, who have him in their midst.

He alone will be capable of carrying the Work of Mary to fulfillment according to the plan he has in his heart.

In the testament of Angela Merici, I found some marvelous passages, where the most outstanding note is that of unity. There we read:

Especially take care that [my daughters] be united and in concord in all they desire, as we read of the Apostles and of the Christians of the early Church: *Erat autem eorum cor unum*— "They were of one heart." . . . And you too must try to be this way with all your daughters, because the more you are united, the more Jesus Christ will be in your midst as a father and good shepherd. . . .

In these my final words to you, I plead with my dying breath that you be in concord, united together, all of one heart and one will. Be bound to one another in the bond of charity, esteeming one another, helping one another, putting up with one another in Jesus Christ. Because if you make the effort to live in this way, without doubt the Lord God will be in your midst.

Therefore, see the importance of this union and concord. Desire it, seek it out, embrace it, hold fast to it with all your might: Because I tell you that if you are all together thus united in heart, you will be like a mighty rock or fortress, invincible against every adversity or persecution or diabolical trickery. Moreover, I tell you that every grace that you ask of God will infallibly be granted.[2]

We have already mentioned that prayer in common is higher that individual prayer. The Curé of Ars said that in the evening, before going to bed, we must pray together, because "where two or three are gathered in my name, there am I in the midst of them."[3]

St. Therese of Lisieux wrote:

I dearly love common prayer, because Jesus promised to be present in the midst of those who meet together in his name; and so I feel that the fervor of my sisters makes up for what is lacking in mine.

She also says:

If our souls are united in him they will be able to save many souls, because our sweet Jesus said: "If two of you agree on earth about anything they ask, it will be done for them" (Mt 18:19).[4]

In the Focolare, whenever we meet together to speak about our great ideal, we usually start out by mentioning a presupposition or better by trying to create a certain reality—we invite everyone present to put aside every personal concern so as to be ready to obtain, all together, the presence of Jesus in the midst. Only after having done this and never before, the meeting begins.

When St. John Bosco called the first general chapter of the Salesians in Lanzo, near Turin, he told them:

Our Divine Savior says in the Gospel that where two or three are gathered together in his name there he is in the midst of them. We have no other aim in our meeting than the glory of God, and the salvation of souls redeemed by the precious blood of Jesus Christ. Therefore we can be certain that the Lord will be in our midst and will manage things in such a way as to bring about great good.[5]

Jesus in the midst and the Councils

Every so often there takes place in the Church a great event, the greatest event—an ecumenical council. Councils were not instituted by God, but, "nevertheless," says Congar, "in the Council there is a certain structure to which the Lord freely united his presence with a formal promise: 'And lo, I am with you always, to the close of the age' (Mt 28:20), and 'Where two or three are gathered in my name, there am I in the midst of them' (Mt 18:20)."

Congar continues:

In this we find a covenant structure (people meet together in the name of Jesus—Jesus becomes present in their midst) comparable, on its own level, to that other structure of more institutional, i.e., juridical form, the covenant structure constituted by the sacraments or by the hierarchical ministries.

This is exactly what the Fathers understood. . . . According to them, where these conditions have been fulfilled and these covenant structures respected, i.e., brotherly love and the fraternal gathering of two or three in his name, the Lord carries out his promise, which in effect is bound to these conditions.[6]

That is, he becomes present.

The Fathers firmly maintain that Jesus is present in the midst of the bishops in Council. As a result, the Council becomes the great hearthfire of the Church, where Jesus extends his light abundantly in order to enlighten the centuries which follow.

Cyril of Alexandria says:

Eagerly following in the footsteps [of the Apostles] those well-known Fathers of ours also met one day in Nicea and defined the venerable and universal symbol of faith.

Certainly together with them sat Christ himself, Christ who said: "Where two or three are gathered in my name, there am I in the midst of them."

How could anyone doubt that Christ invisibly presided over that great and holy synod? In fact it laid the ground, indeed it set down throughout the entire world a basis and foundation that is firm and unshakable—the confession of the true and irreproachable faith. If this is so, how could Christ have been absent, since he himself is the foundation, as the wise words of Paul indicate.[7]

Paul writes: "For no other foundation can any one lay than that which is laid, which is Jesus Christ" (1 Cor 3:11).

John Chrysostom, in one of his correspondences, writes:

> Be careful of what you are doing when you condemn such illustrious Fathers (of the Council of Nicea), such courageous and wise Fathers. . . .
>
> Do you not know the words of Christ: "Where two or three are gathered in my name, there am I in the midst of them"? Because, if where there are two or three Christ is in their midst, with all the more reason where there were three hundred and many more, he was present disposing and deciding everything.[8]

Similarly, in every true focolare center we are certain that the one who decides and disposes everything is he. In fact, we do not feel we are doing the will of a man or a woman when we are given some task, but the will of Jesus in the midst. And this makes us aware that we are living in the freedom of the sons of God.

Leontius writes:

> In the Council, you say, a few people were present who were well known to have once favored Nestorius. . . .
>
> How . . . because of the presence of two or three members of wrong faith, whose impious thoughts were unknown to the others, will the entire venerable assembly and the sacred synod

of 630 prelates, as if they were all impious, be abandoned by God and thus be unable to discern the truth, especially when God himself promised: "Where two or three are gathered in my name, there am I in the midst of them?"[9]

John of Damascus writes:

Regarding these matters the decision does not rest on emperors, but on the Councils, just as our Lord said: "Where two or three are gathered in my name, there am I in the midst of them."[10]

Isn't it encouraging for us, and a cause of enthusiasm, that the greatest event of the Church has the very structure that God gave to us little children of the Church? How beautiful and consoling it is to find we are the image of such a mother.

Vatican II on Jesus in the midst

Now let's take a look at the Second Vatican Council, which God willed should take place during our lifetimes.

It, too, was certainly guided by Jesus in the midst of the Fathers.

But since for us, who live in this century, it is of the greatest importance to see whether the charism that moves us is in harmony with the spirit of the entire present-day Church, let's glance through the pages of the Council texts to see whether it speaks explicitly about Jesus in the midst.

We have seen that it does. Fr. Foresi, in his book *Reaching for More*, says:

Until the Second Vatican Council, the passage in the Gospel, "Where two or three are gathered together in my name, there am I in the midst of them," was rarely ever mentioned.

If one excludes the Council of Chalcedon,[11] one will find that throughout the whole history of the Church, even in the most solemn conciliar documents, this phrase is hardly ever quoted.

The Second Vatican Council, however, did not produce a

single document which does not point toward this fundamental idea. . . .

We can certainly say that this idea was the soul of the Council, especially present in the Council's statement on collegiality (cf. *Lumen Gentium*, c. III).[12]

Vatican II speaks of Jesus in the midst in the Constitution on the Sacred Liturgy. After enumerating the various ways Christ is present in the life of the Church, it says, "Lastly, he is present when the Church prays and sings, for he has promised 'Where two or three are gathered together in my name, there am I in the midst of them' (Mt 18:20)."[13]

We find it spoken of in a splendid way in the Decree on the Renewal of Religious Life. When we read this passage, we understand why the Work of Mary had to give birth to the branch of men and women religious. The charism God gave us is brimming over with these ideas, with these truths. This charism could be of help to many religious who might not know how to put the words of the Council into practice, or who, in times of religious crises like these, might no longer understand the meaning of religious life. The Council says:

> Common life in prayer and the sharing of the same spirit (Acts 2:42), should be constant, after the example of the early Church, in which the company of believers were of one heart and soul. It should be nourished by the teaching of the Gospel and by the sacred liturgy, especially by the Eucharist. Religious, as members of Christ, should live together as brothers and should give pride of place to one another in esteem (cf. Rom 12:10), carrying one another's burdens (cf. Gal 6:12). A community gathered together as a true family in the Lord's name enjoys his presence (cf. Mt 18:20), through the love of God which is poured into their hearts by the Holy Spirit (cf. Rom 5:5). For love sums up the law (cf. Rom 13:10) and is the bond which makes us perfect (cf. Col 3:14); by it we know that we have crossed over from death to life (cf. 1 Jn 3:14). Indeed, the unity of the brethren is a symbol of the coming of Christ (cf. Jn 13:35; 17:21) and is a source of great apostolic power."[14]

The Second Vatican Council mentions Jesus in the midst again in the Decree on the Apostolate of the laity, when it speaks of individual apostolate, saying that it is useful especially in those places where the freedom of the Church is hampered, and suggesting in any case that they

> can gather for discussion into small groups with no rigid form of rules or organization. . . . It ensures the continual presence before the eyes of others of a sign of the Church's community, a sign that will be seen as a genuine witness of love.[15]

Then in speaking about group apostolate, it emphasizes the line of action that God gave to our Work as well. After affirming that "Where two or three are gathered together in my name, there am I in the midst of them," it says: "For that reason Christians will exercise their apostolate in a spirit of concord."[16]

In the same Decree, among the principal fields of lay apostolic activity, the first two to be mentioned are that of the parish, which "offers an outstanding example of community apostolate" and that of the family.[17]

Here we would want to stop and praise God for having led us to found the New Parish Movement and the New Families Movement.

Is it not evident that it is Jesus in the midst who leads us on, the same Jesus who presided over the recent Council?

Finally, the Council speaks about Jesus in the midst in the Decree on Ecumenism, inviting the faithful—in order to bring about the union of Christians—to lead a life according to the Gospel, and to use the *consenserint* to beseech the grace of unity among separated brothers, "because where two or three are gathered together in my name, there am I in the midst of them" (Mt 18:20).[18]

In this area too, we feel that our vocation is surprisingly up to date. With our effort to live the Gospel we are moving along these lines, and since we cannot be united through the Eucharist with a good part of the separated churches, we feel we can be united, if the necessary conditions are fulfilled, by the presence of Jesus among two or more. This is our ecumenism.

Paul VI on Jesus in the midst

To conclude, we wanted to find out if Pope Paul VI himself has made mention of Jesus in the midst. We see that he has spoken about it a number of times: to the Cardinals in the Consistory of 1969, to the Italian Bishops' Conference, to the pastors and lenten preachers of Rome, and on other occasions besides.

A splendid example is what the pope said on his visit to the parish of Our Lady, Comforter of the Afflicted:

> Are the faithful united in love, in the charity of Christ? Then certainly this is a living parish, here is the true Church, since then there is a flourishing of that divine and human phenomenon which perpetuates the presence of Christ among us. Or are the faithful together only because they are listed in the parish register or recorded in the baptismal files? Do they gather only to hear Mass on Sunday, without getting to know one another, maybe even elbowing one another out of the way? If so, the Church in this case does not appear bound together; the cement, which must bind all members into a real, organic unity, is not yet at work. . . .
>
> Remember, the solemn words of Christ: They will truly recognize you as my disciples, as authentic, faithful followers, if you love one another, if there is this warmth of affection and sentiment; if there is a vibrant sympathy for others—a sympathy not merely passively experienced but deliberately willed, not merely spontaneously arising but purposely achieved, with that breadth of heart and power of begetting Jesus in our midst which spring from awareness of our unity in him and through him.[19]

And so, if the "true Church" is like this, then we must conclude that from every side we are challenged to do whatever is possible on our part, on our movement's part, to make this Church shine out with the presence of Jesus amidst the lives of people in as many places as possible.

PART III

WHEN DID WE SEE YOU LORD?

MADE IN GOD'S IMAGE

In the course of this section I intend to consider in depth the true nature of that extraordinary being, the human being. I hope to bring out the riches that are to be found in every human being, and to discover God's plan for each person we meet, as this affects his or her relationship with each one of us.

The experience of our movement

Our movement has always had an enormous respect for every human being. From the very beginning, we used to say with great conviction that we cannot go to God alone, but we must go to him with our brothers and sisters, since he is the Father of us all.

Initially, in our special concern for the poor (though without overlooking others), and later, in our contact with everyone, we discovered how much each person enriched our lives; and we realized that, in the Focolare, after God, for God, and with God, our neighbor has first place.

The fact is that the Focolare has always tried to live the essence of the Christian message. For this reason, when someone asks what the basic teachings of the movement are, we respond with the same words Jesus used in answering the Pharisees: "You shall love the Lord your God with all your heart, and with all your soul, and with all your mind. . . . You shall love your neighbor as yourself" (Mt 22:37-39).

It is through our neighbor that we continually pass from an empty and meaningless life to a full life: "We have passed out of death into life, because we love the brethren" (1 Jn 3:14).

When we love our neighbor, we notice that our union with God grows.

With our neighbor we can already begin here on earth to pattern our lives on the life of the Trinity; we can erect a temple of God in the midst of the world; and we can experience a foretaste of heaven in this life.

In the Focolare we do not use extraordinary means of mortification because in loving our neighbor and making ourselves one with him or her—which requires the silence or death of our own ego—we have found a way to demolish our old self and allow our new self to live.

All this is possible because in one way or another, Christ renders himself present in every human being: in everyone we meet, we meet the Lord.

Anyone who observes the life of the Focolare from without can clearly see how this aspect is understood and lived. Recently, for example, a prominent Catholic remarked that in our spirituality we take our neighbor "incredibly seriously." In the Focolare, he said, one does not only find that attitude of human solidarity which is so stressed in the various secular and Marxist humanisms of our day; nor does one merely encounter a fraternal solidarity based on our "common destiny" (currently a much-used expression in several parts of the world). No. The Focolare, he continued, has emphasized that each of our fellow human beings is not merely a relative or a co-worker, a companion in joy or someone entrusted to our care, and still less a rival in battle. Every person is an individual loved by Jesus, and in whom Jesus—who is always present, though in different ways in different persons—must take shape. In each person I meet, Jesus comes to me: as a gift, an enrichment, an encouragement, a purification; and in each person, Jesus wants to be loved and served.

The anthropological trend in theology, he continued, has centered its attention on the human person utilizing the findings of moderns psychology, sociology and education, which must not be underestimated. These theological efforts have certainly produced valuable contributions, but in the final analysis, he said, it is revelation which must determine anthropology.

He concluded by saying that the Focolare also focuses its attention on the human person but in the right way: according to revelation.

The members of the Focolare, with God's grace, continually try to love those around them, even in the most insignificant circumstances of life. Whenever they forget to do so, they begin again, with that complete concern for the other's needs which is the best antidote for egoism. They show by their actions that love of neighbor is not an unattainable ideal—provided that one desires to relive the life of Jesus today. As a consequence, since the flame of this supernatural love is difficult to resist, it has grown into a blazing fire.

We went out to love our brothers and sisters first in Trent, then throughout Italy, Europe, and the world. From person to person, a vast network of love was spread over the earth among people of all ages, vocations, and social backgrounds.

And with ever-increasing intensity we continued, keeping up as much as possible with what was happening everywhere else in the world, and—on a more intimate level—sharing the sufferings that cause Jesus to grow in each one of us: all for one, and one for all.

Beginning in 1960, God put us in contact not only with our fellow Catholics, but with our Christian brothers and sisters in other Churches and denominations. And since 1976, we have come into more direct contact with our brothers and sisters of other religions, or—to speak more generically—with those who do not know Jesus.

We did not stop in the face of this more difficult responsibility, because God's grace quickly spurred us on to a sincere and enthusiastic love for these immense portions of humanity.

I recently heard someone refer to this aspect of the Work of Mary as a continuation of the episode of the visitation, in which Mary sets out "with haste" to visit Elizabeth, in spite of the distance which separates them. She who was full of grace set out to visit her cousin, bearing Jesus in her womb. She was also bringing Jesus to the one who was to be his precursor, in order that he might be sanctified. But in bringing Jesus, Mary understood even more profoundly the mystery that had been entrusted to her, and she expressed it in the "Magnificat" (Lk 1:46-55).

The movement offers itself—and this is the life style of the entire Church—so that it might become a means of encounter between Jesus and his present-day precursors, so to speak; that is, between Jesus in Christians and those "seeds of the Word" which are present in the believers of the various other religions. Like the Church, the Focolare also wants to be a means of encounter between Jesus and the hearts and minds of those who reject God, but who—because they are made in his image, and because the human soul is naturally Christian—still tend unconsciously toward this meeting with the Lord.

As the members of the Focolare hasten toward these new brothers and sisters, a new light is enkindled in their minds, and they realize the greatness of the vocation to which the Focolare has been called. And in their hearts they utter a small "Magnificat."

But who are these persons whom we have rushed out to meet, or whom we desire to encounter?

If we look at the words of Scripture we will find an answer, and we will understand more deeply what the Holy Spirit has been, and still is, prompting us to do.

The Old Testament view

Let us go back to the book of Genesis: "Then God said, 'Let us make man in our image, after our likeness . . .' So God created man in his own image" (Gn 1:26-27). This passage does not so much tell us what a human being is, as what God intended to do and did; that is, it tells us who we are according to God's creative purpose. The decision to create humankind and its actual creation in God's image are tightly bound to one another. These words of Genesis tell us that the Creator set out to create someone who would have a relationship with him.

86

Unlike all other created beings, including the animals, which Genesis says were created "according to their kinds" (Gn 1:25), only human beings are created "in the image of God" (Gn 1:27). We, therefore, are the only creatures who have a direct, personal relationship with God: we stand before him, his "you." This special relationship with God is what constitutes being human. "The relationship with God is not something added to human nature, rather man is created such that his human nature is understood within his relationship with God."[1]

This is stupendous! And it is true! Does not humankind itself "call for" the existence of God, thereby becoming the greatest witness to God's existence? Do not human beings alone—in contrast to all the other beings on earth—feel in their hearts a desire for something or someone transcendent, and a longing for what is infinite and immortal?

And when they fail to find a solution to the innumerable problems that the universe presents, do they not lift their gaze in search of Someone who must be there because he cannot *not* be there? Yes, this is how human beings act when they are pure and sincere.

Moreover, if human life only has meaning in the context of a relationship with God, then religion is not just one aspect of life; rather, it must involve the whole of it.

Thank you, God, for the ideal you have given us! For that is what you have taught us: that religion must involve everything else.

For people in today's world, this is a revolution. But you have told us that the twenty-four hours of every day must be for you. You are the one who wants our whole heart, our whole mind, our whole strength. And even when we are loving or thinking about or doing something for someone other than you, it is still for you and in you that we must love, think, and act.

"God said 'Let us make man in our image, after our likeness' " (Gn 1:26). Commenting on this passage, Irenaeus, bishop of Lyons, wrote:

> Angels had no power to make an image of God, nor [did] anyone else. . . . God did not stand in need of these beings in

order to accomplish what He had Himself determined . . . should be done. . . . For with Him were always present . . . the Son and the Spirit . . . to whom He speaks, saying, "Let us make man after our image and likeness" (Gn 1:26).[2]

How true this interpretation seems to me! For when God created the human person, he created humankind as a whole, as "someone" who stands before him. And if humanity wished to be as God wants it to be, it must be in the image of God, who is one and triune. Human beings must live in a relationship of love with one another as do the persons of the Trinity, in whose image they have been created.

Furthermore, if in creating the human being, God created all people and placed them in this relationship with him, then each and every person is called to this relationship regardless of the diversity in human nature, regardless of differences in religious belief, and regardless of whether one is a believer or not.

The Second Vatican Council also interprets the passage, "in the image of God he created him; male and female he created them" (Gn 1:27), as meaning that to be made in God's image involves a special relationship with God: human beings have the capacity to know and love God. This is true not only in the sense that, since each human person is made in God's likeness, he or she is capable of having a rapport with him, but in an even stronger sense: human beings are capable of knowing and loving like God—God, the only being whose very nature is to know and to love.

Gregory of Nyssa affirms:

> God is also love and the source of love . . . the Creator has made this our characteristic as well. . . . Therefore, if love is lacking, the entire character of the image is altered.[3]

John Chrysostom tells us how this image is to be treated:

> How many men have not only cast down, but also trodden underfoot the images of God! For when you throttle a debtor, when you strip him, when you drag him away, you trample

underfoot God's image. . . . But if you say that man is not of the same substance as God—what does that matter? . . . If men are not of the same substance as God, . . . still they have been called His image; and it is fitting they should receive honor on that account.[4]

Sin has not caused this image to be destroyed or lost. Origen declares: "The image of God remains in you always, even though you cover it with the image of the earthly man."[5]

However, even though it has not been destroyed by sin, it has been disfigured. Thus we have the coming of Jesus, who restores us to God's image. Augustine says: "Man was made in God's image and likeness, and he defaced it by sin. His true and lasting good therefore will be assured if this [image] is stamped anew [by Baptism]."[6]

Irenaeus affirms that it is necessary to be "grafted" into the Word of God in order to live in the image and likeness of God:

> St. Paul says, "But you, being a wild olive-tree, have been grafted into the good olive-tree, and have been made a partaker of the richness of the olive-tree" (Rom 11:17-24). . . . [In the same way] those persons who are not bringing forth the fruits of righteousness, and are, as it were, covered over and lost among brambles, if they use diligence and receive the word of God as a graft, arrive at the original nature of man—that which was created after the image and likeness of God.[7]

Finally, Paul VI sees in Mary "the woman, the true woman who is ideal and real, the person in whom the image of God is reflected with absolute clarity."[8] And he urges Christians to imitate her:

> It is impossible to honor her who is "full of grace" (Lk 1:28) without thereby honoring in oneself the state of grace, which is friendship with God, communion with him, and the indwelling of the Holy Spirit. It is this divine grace which takes possession of the whole man and conforms him to the image of the Son of God. . . . Mary, the New Woman, stands at the side of Christ, the

New Man, within whose mystery alone, the mystery of man finds true light.[9]

Persons created by God

Although the Old Testament expresses the greatness and dignity of human nature by revealing that human beings are made in God's image, nonetheless, it stresses above all that they are created, created by God.

Therefore, insofar as they are created, their being is radically different from that of their Creator, and they are totally dependent on him for their existence. "A living relationship with God is always essential to full human existence. The godless person is considered lost . . . perverted in his or her very being."[10]

Persons to be loved

In the Old Testament human beings are presented as persons who are to be treated with love. In Leviticus, God commands:

> You shall not hate your brother in your heart, but you shall reason with your neighbor, lest you bear sin because of him. You shall not take vengeance or bear any grudge against the sons of your own people, but you shall love your neighbor as yourself: I am the Lord. . . .
> The stranger who sojourns with you shall be to you as the native among you, and you shall love him as yourself; for you were strangers in the land of Egypt. (Lv 19:17-18, 34)

Worship, ritual, and the prophets

Worship and ritual were desired and established by God, as described elsewhere in Leviticus. But when the Jewish people believed they were satisfying him by simply performing the prescribed rites, then God sent the prophets who called them back to an interior conversion that was to be expressed in love of one's neighbor as a witness of one's love for God. For we can see that whenever God's law was scorned in human relationships, and God himself was sought after only in ritual forms of worship, then God was reduced to "an impersonal source of magical power, which can be manipulated with no feeling of reverence whatsoever simply by means of a meticulous routine."[11]

When they saw that by means of such rituals religion was being falsified at its very heart, the prophets had no choice but to repudiate these ritual observances, which had aroused God's judgment and indignation:

> I hate, I despise your feasts, and I take no delight in your solemn assemblies. Even though you offer me your burnt offerings . . . I will not accept them. . . . Take away from me the noise of your songs; to the melody of your harps I will not listen. But let justice roll down like water, and righteousness like an everflowing stream. (Am 5:21-24)
>
> The Lord has a controversy with the inhabitants of the land. There is no faithfulness or kindness . . . there is swearing, lying, killing, stealing, and committing adultery; they break all bounds and murder follows murder. Therefore the land mourns, and all who dwell in it languish. (Hos 6:6)
>
> When you spread forth your hands, I will hide my eyes from you; even though you make many prayers, I will not listen. . . . Learn to do good; seek justice, correct oppression; defend the fatherless, plead for the widow. (Is 1:15, 17)

This controversy concerning worship and ritual shows that

> the right relationship with God is determined by means of the right relationship with our fellow human beings and that the service of the divine liturgy must always be accompanied by the service of our fellow men and women.[12]

In the final analysis, what the prophets were actually coming out so strongly against was

> a perversion of meaning which has threatened all human worship through the centuries: sacrifice, worship, and prayer only keep their true sense as long as in them men are really concerned to

91

encounter the holy God. If man tries to make use of them to give himself security in the sight of God, then they become a blasphemy; sacrifice becomes a means of self-justification, the celebration of feasts the occasion of mere emotional exaltation, and prayer, a meaningless, craven, or hypocritical wailing.[13]

The fasting which pleases God: love of neighbor

God does not even like the observance of fasting when it is not linked to love for one's neighbor, as he shows in Isaiah:

> Cry aloud, spare not, lift up your voice like a trumpet; declare to my people their transgression. . . . Behold, you fast only to quarrel and to fight and to hit with wicked fist. Fasting like yours this day will not make your voice to be heard on high. Is such the fast that I choose, a day for a man to humble himself? Is it to bow his head like a rush, and to spread sackcloth and ashes under him? Will you call this a fast, and a day acceptable to the Lord?
>
> Is not this the fast that I choose: to loose the bonds of wickedness, to undo the thongs of the yoke, to let the oppressed go free, and to break every yoke? Is it not to share your bread with the hungry, and bring the homeless poor into your house; when you see the naked, to cover him, and not to hide yourself from your own flesh? . . . Then you shall call, and the Lord will answer; you shall cry, and he will say, Here I am. (Is 58:1, 4-7, 9; see also Is 59)

After such a severe criticism of the abuse of fast days, one would expect the rites themselves to be confirmed as being holy. Yet the opposite occurs. Though not questioning the practice of fast days as such, the prophet radically challenges the accompanying practices (humbling oneself, bowing one's head, using sackcloth and ashes, etc.). The fasting which pleases God consists in replacing actions directed towards God with actions directed towards one's neighbor. In so doing, one is truly mortifying oneself, and offering God another kind of fasting.

Among the various acts of this sort, one is particularly pleasing to God: loosing the bonds of injustice and freeing the oppressed. The experience of exile and slavery in Egypt, followed by the experience of being liberated by God, had given Israel a new appreciation of the meaning of freedom.

The other acts listed by the prophet are the traditional acts of assistance to those in need. We are presented with a panorama of those least-regarded by society: the poor, the outcasts, slaves, prisoners, the hungry, the homeless, those dressed in rags. The picture is similar to that of the Last Judgment (cf. Mt 25:35-36). God says to come to their assistance "and not to hide yourself (pretending not to notice [cf. Dt 22:1]) from your own flesh" (Is 58:7); that is, from your own flesh and blood, which can be interpreted as referring to every human being, and not merely those of our own country—which was the general interpretation among the Jews (cf. Jb 31:15).[14]

How beautiful are the words of Job:

> I delivered the poor who cried, and the fatherless who had none to help him. The blessing of him who was about to perish came upon me, and I caused the widow's heart to sing for joy. . . . I was eyes to the blind, and feet to the lame. I was a father to the poor, and I searched out the cause of him whom I did not know. (Jb 29:12-13, 15-16)

If we perform the deeds which constitute a "fast" acceptable to the Lord, then we will experience blessings.

Love for enemies

Lastly, the Old Testament is not lacking in references to loving one's enemies:

> If your enemy is hungry, give him bread to eat; and if he is thirsty give him water to drink; for you will heap coals of fire on his head, and the Lord will reward you. (Prv 25:21-22; see also Sir 28:1-9)

JESUS' PRESENCE IN THE CHRISTIAN AS PRESENTED IN THE NEW TESTAMENT

If we read the New Testament—particularly the four Gospels, the letters of Paul, and the first letter of John—we find clear and often stupendous affirmations of the presence of Jesus in our neighbor.

The Gospels

Let us begin with the Gospels. In some passages Jesus identifies himself with the apostles or with those he has sent out; in others, with his followers; and in still others, with every human being. This identification can be understood from the contexts in which Jesus is speaking.

Jesus present in the apostles

Jesus' presence in his apostles is affirmed in all four Gospels, with illustrations that range from giving them a welcome that is more than mere hospitality, to listening to them. For example:

> He who receives you receives me, and he who receives me receives him who sent me. (Mt 10:40)
> He who hears you hears me, and he who rejects you rejects me, and he who rejects me rejects him who sent me. (Lk 10:16)
> Truly, truly, I say to you, he who receives anyone whom I send receives me; and he who receives me receives him who sent me. (Jn 13:20)

94

In this missionary context, Jesus also identifies himself with a "child" and with "little ones" (Mk 9:37; Mt 10:42), but it is probable that these words are also meant to indicate those he is sending out. For among those sent out by Jesus there were some who did not enjoy the esteem of the people; in fact, they might even have been treated with contempt. So Jesus speaks out in their behalf. He wants to inspire love for them in the Christian communities, and he wants his followers to do the same. For however weak or mediocre his messengers may be, they bring his word. In the Old Testament, in fact, the messenger was considered the mouth of the one who had sent him (cf. Jer 15:19); and according to Jewish tradition the emissary (*shaliah*) of a person is like the person himself.

We can presume, therefore, that in using the words which have come down to us as "child" in Mark and "little ones" in Matthew, Jesus was referring to those he was sending out as his emissaries:

> Whoever receives one such child in my name receives me; and whoever receives me, receives not me but him who sent me. (Mk 9:37)
>
> And whoever gives to one of these little ones even a cup of cold water because he is a disciple, truly, I say to you, he shall not lose his reward. (Mt 10:42)

This presence of Jesus in his apostles, in those he has sent as his emissaries, receives a new value after his death and resurrection. For after the resurrection, the apostles are incorporated into Christ, and he is actually mystically present in them. Their word is then efficacious of itself, and not only because they have been charged with passing it on. Jesus is acting in them; therefore, whoever receives one of the apostles after Jesus' resurrection experiences a real encounter with him. Paul, too, stresses this on various occasions.

> You received me as an angel of God, as Christ Jesus. (Gal 4:14)
>
> When you received the word of God which you heard from us, you accepted it not as the word of men but as what it really

is, the word of God, which is at work in you believers. (1 Thess 2:13)

So we are ambassadors for Christ, God making his appeal through us. (2 Cor 5:20) You desire proof that Christ is speaking in me. (2 Cor 13:3)

Jesus present in the disciples

The Gospels also give us affirmations of the presence of Jesus in the ordinary Christian, in the context of the life of the community formed by his disciples. Words such as "who receives you, receives me," originally referring only to those sent out by Jesus, are later generalized and applied to the relationships between the members of the Christian community, particularly with regard to those in need. Love directed toward the least and the neediest of one's brothers and sisters must be considered as love for Jesus in person. For example Luke relates this episode:

> And an argument arose among them as to which of them was the greatest. But when Jesus perceived the thought of their hearts, he took a child and put him by his side, and said to them, "Whoever receives this child in my name receives him who sent me; for he who is least among you all is the one who is great." (Lk 9:46-48)

In this instance, as in so many others, Jesus completely overturns the normal scale of values: that which other people treat with contempt, he puts in a position of prominence. As a consequence, for Christians, the poorest and the least are in reality the greatest and the most important, because Jesus has put himself on their side—so much so, that whoever receives one such person receives Jesus himself.[1]

We are dealing here with relationships between Christians, wherein the motivation for loving is consciously supernatural. For Jesus says that the person must be received "in my name": with full knowledge, therefore, of what one is doing, and with the intention of following the Lord's teaching. Jesus' entire life is an extraordinary and wonderful lesson on how to treat those in need.

Jesus' solidarity with all his followers without distinction, but particularly with those who are suffering, is also expressed in the words addressed to Saul outside Damascus, as he was heading there to arrest the Christians: "'Saul, Saul, why do you persecute me?' And he said, 'Who are you, Lord?' And he said, 'I am Jesus, whom you are persecuting' " (Acts 9:4-5).

Jesus present in every person

In the Gospels we also find affirmations of the presence of Jesus in every human being. We need only call to mind the cosmic vision of the Last Judgment, which concludes with the affirmation: " . . . as you did it to one of the least of these my brethren, you did it to me" (Mt 25:40). But we will consider this presence of Jesus in a later chapter.

The letters of Paul

Jesus' presence in those who believe

Let us now look at what Paul's letters have to say about the presence of Christ in the Christian. Rather than speak of Christ in the believer, Paul generally prefers another expression: to be "in Christ," by which he wants to indicate the believer's incorporation into Christ's body, the Church, which has taken place at baptism. This expression occurs 164 times in his letters.

This reality of unity, this communitarian aspect brought out by our being "in Christ," is also expressed with the words "Christ in": "Here there cannot be Greek or Jew. . . slave, free man, but Christ is all, and in all" (Col 3:11). What Paul is emphasizing here is that Christ, who is present in each of us, has made us all members of his body. Since Christ has placed us in this unity, which is himself, we are all brothers and sisters, irrespective of all previous differences of race, nationality, social standing, or other perceived barriers.

This being "in Christ" simultaneously brings about a personal unity between the Christian and Jesus, a union so profound that it creates in the Christian a new "self." For Paul, in fact, the presence of Jesus in the believer is a mystical identification: the believer becomes one being with Christ. ("Identification" here signifies a very profound union, which has no parallel on the natural-human level; a union, however, in which the distinction between the persons is preserved.)

When Paul affirms, "It is no longer I who live, but Christ who lives in me" (Gal 2:20), he is not speaking merely of a mystical experience he has had, but of that identification of the believer with Christ which is the totally new thing about being a Christian, and which has made him a new person.

This indwelling of Christ in the believer gives rise to a marvelous consequence: Christians need no longer be anxious about seeking self-fulfillment or planning out their future. They have only to adhere to Christ living in them, who will gradually reveal his plan for each individual and will guide him or her through a great divine adventure, hitherto unknown.

This is what all the members of the Focolare have set out to do, once they have discovered its particular charism, which, seen in this light, is nothing other than a new understanding of Christianity—new, because it has been revived by the Spirit.

The believer "with" Christ

This identification of the Christian with Jesus certainly does not mean that the believer is absorbed by him. What it implies is a communion of life, and therefore dialogue, dynamism, growth, "until"—as Paul says—"Christ be formed in you" (Gal 4:19).

In order to express this mysterious sharing in the life of Jesus, Paul uses the expression "to be with Christ." In fact, he coins new verbs with the Greek prefix *syn* ("with," "together") in order to show that the Christian's life conforms to the life of Christ: it is an experience of death and resurrection.

> You were *buried with him* in baptism, in which you were also *raised with him*. (Col 2:12)

Our old self was *crucified with him*. (Rom 6:6)
If we *have died with him*, we shall also *live with him*. (2 Tm 2:11)
We *have died with him*, we shall also *live with him* in a death like his. (Rom 6:5)
God . . . made us *alive together with Christ*. (Eph 2:4-5)

From this perspective as well, we have seen that the life of the members of the Focolare as a whole retraces the footsteps of Jesus: in his joy and his suffering, his successes and his abandonment, and in that glory which is compatible with our earthly life.

The bond between Christianity and the New Covenant

We could cite many other passages of Paul regarding the presence of Jesus in the believer. However, I would now like to focus on the way Paul frequently connects the reality brought by Jesus with the great promise of the Spirit's presence in human hearts (Rom 8; 1 Thes 4:9), which we find in Jeremiah and Ezekiel as a characteristic of the New Covenant:

> But this is the covenant which I will make with the house of Israel those days, says the Lord: I will put my law within them, and I will write it upon their hearts; and I will be their God, and they shall be my people. And no longer shall each man teach his neighbor . . . for they shall all know me, from the least of them to the greatest, says the Lord. (Jer 31:33-34)

Ezekiel identifies the law written in their hearts, which Jeremiah speaks of, with the very Spirit of God: "And I will put my spirit within you, and cause you to walk in my statutes and be careful to observe my ordinances" (Ez 36:27).

Precisely because of this indwelling of God in the Christian, he or she is no longer obeying or disobeying a commandment, even one which is God-given, but is either submitting to or directly opposing "God's activity in the very heart of the Christian through the gift of His Spirit."[2]

Paul sees all this fulfilled in the Christian community: "But concerning love of the brethren you have no need to have any one write to you, for you yourselves have been taught by God to love one another" (1 Thes 4:9).

Therefore, the presence of Christ in the heart of the believer by means of the Spirit is the accomplishment of the definitive, eschatological presence of God in humanity and in the Church.

The relationship and the difference between the presence of Jesus and the presence of the Holy Spirit

The presence of the Spirit in the Christian and the presence of Jesus in the Christian are inseparably bound to one another. To have the Spirit signifies that one belongs to Christ. Christ gives himself to the believer in the Spirit.

The theologian Durrwell shows the difference between these two presences very well:

> Christ is present in the faithful. Also, "God has sent the spirit of his Son into your hearts" (Gal 4:6). But each of these guests is established in us in his own fashion. . . . Whereas the Spirit is *given* to us . . . we *are* the body of Christ. Whereas our bodies are the temple of the Spirit, they are the members of Christ! (1 Cor 6:15, 19). The Spirit dwells in Christ and in us who are the body of Christ. The guest is not confused with the house in which he dwells. Though filling all things, the Spirit does not identify the faithful with himself.[3]

But Christ does.

Jesus in the believer according to John

John, like Paul, has his own way of speaking about the presence of Jesus in the Christian. His characteristic formula is: the believer in Christ, and Christ in the believer. For John, therefore, this indwelling is mutual.

In his Gospel he speaks of it with reference to the Eucharist: "He who eats my flesh and drinks my blood abides in me and I in him" (Jn 6:56). The word "abide" is consoling because it gives the idea of a mutual immanence that is not momentary, but permanent. Therefore, we can be in union with Christ the whole day long. And this union is a profound interpenetration which has no parallel on the human level.

John speaks of this immanence again when he gives the very appropriate example of the vine and the branches:

> I am the vine, you are the branches. He who abides in me, and I in him . . . bears much fruit, for apart from me you can do nothing. . . . If you abide in me, and my words abide in you, ask whatever you will, and it shall be done for you. (15:5, 7)

And he speaks of it again in the seventeenth chapter where he says, for example, "I in them and you in me, that they may become perfectly one" (verse 23).

John does not speak only of the presence of Christ in the believer; but he states explicitly that the Trinity itself comes to dwell in the Christian. Let us look, for example, at chapter 14:15-23.

The first part deals with the presence of the Holy Spirit in the believers. His coming is linked to the departure of Jesus, and his role is to render Jesus present in them. Before Jesus' death, in fact, his disciples remained outside of him, so to speak. But after the resurrection, the action of the Holy Spirit brings about the presence of the glorified Christ within the believer. From this comes the new relationship of the believer with Jesus:

> I will pray the Father, and he will give you another Counselor, to be with you forever, the Spirit of truth, whom the world cannot receive, because it neither sees him nor knows him; you know him, for he dwells with you, and will be in you. (14:16-17)

In the second part, John says that it is a characteristic of the risen Christ to be with the Father, and that through Christ the believer can also be with the Father, in a new relationship with him:

> I will not leave you desolate; I will come to you. . . . On that day you will know that I am in the Father, and you in me, and I in you. (14:18, 20)

In the third part we find the condition set by Jesus for his presence in the believer: faithfulness to his commandments, which leads to a deeper understanding of God. If this condition is met, the Trinity will come to dwell in the believer:

> He who has my commandments and keeps them, he it is who loves me; and he who loves me will be loved by my father, and I will love him and manifest myself to him. . . . If a man loves me, he will keep my word, and my Father will love him, and we will come to him and make our home with him. (14:21, 23)

M. J. Lagrange comments on this moving final verse:

> Nothing is demanded by way of intellectual culture, tendency toward contemplation, or some special asceticism. . . . God does not come to call forth ecstasy or any other outward manifestation. He comes to dwell in the heart of the one who loves him. Nothing could be simpler as an expression of this mysticism, and nothing could be more profound.[4]

John not only affirms this mutual indwelling in his Gospel, but also in his first letter—but with a variation: instead of speaking of Jesus he speaks of God (cf. 1 Jn 3:24). The content does not change, however, because the presence of God implies the presence of Christ, and in this letter John asserts in a unique way that Jesus Christ is God.

He also reiterates and clarifies the condition under which God remains in us and we in God: that we keep God's commandments. And these he reduces to two: believe in Jesus, and love one another (cf. 1 Jn 3:23).

Furthermore, he states that the Spirit who moves us to confess our faith in Jesus and to love each other is the same Spirit who guarantees that God lives in us (cf. 1 Jn 3:23-24).

At this point I cannot go on without giving special thanks to God. Everyone who knows the Focolare's history knows that at the beginning the first Focolarine decided to live the New Commandment, and that all who have begun to live this spirituality since then have made the same decision. Now John explains who it was who urged us to choose that particular commandment, and instilled in our hearts such a great faith in the Gospel. It was the Holy Spirit. Let us give him thanks forever.

And another joyous observation: if we believed and if we loved one another, then Christ was in us and we in him. May he always keep it this way!

Now allow me to conclude this brief examination of the presence of God (or Christ) in the believer, by turning to the revelation central to Christianity: God is love.

John says that "God is love, and he who abides in love abides in God, and God abides in him" (1 Jn 4:16), because love, reciprocal love, which presupposes faith, is the condition for remaining in communion with God.

And God who is Love is the immense sun which has enlightened and continues to enlighten all those who encounter the Focolare. God who is Love: for us—as for others—he was, is, and will always be the starting point and foundation of our entire Christian life.

And finally, here is a verse from the book of Revelation (the Apocalypse), also the work of John, which beautifully shows again that God is love and that, as such, he dwells in us. These words should fill our hearts with joy: "Behold, I stand at the door and knock; if any one hears my voice and opens the door, I will come in to him and eat with him, and he with me" (Rv 3:20). To eat with Jesus: yes, for when one experiences the profound happiness of that intimate conversation with God, it is like sharing a banquet of love with him.

JESUS IN THOSE WHO SUFFER

The Last Judgment

I think it is appropriate to read now, in its entirety, the passage describing the most awe-inspiring and momentous event that all of us will one day have to experience:

> When the Son of man comes in his glory, and all the angels with him, then he will sit on his glorious throne. Before him will be gathered all the nations, and he will separate them one from another as a shepherd separates the sheep from the goats, and he will place the sheep at his right hand, but the goats at the left. Then the King will say to those at his right hand, "Come, O blessed of my Father, inherit the kingdom prepared for you from the foundation of the world; for I was hungry and you gave me food, I was thirsty and you gave me drink, I was a stranger and you welcomed me, I was naked and you clothed me, I was sick and you visited me, I was in prison and you came to me." Then the righteous will answer him, "Lord, when did we see you hungry and feed you, or thirsty and give you drink? And when did we see you a stranger and welcome you, or naked and clothe you? And when did we see you sick or in prison and visit you?" And the King will answer them, "Truly, I say to you, as you did it to one of the least of these my brethren, you did it to me." Then he will say to those at his left hand, "Depart from me, you cursed, into the eternal fire prepared for the devil and his angels; for I was hungry and you gave me no food, I was thirsty and you gave me no drink, I was a stranger and you did not welcome me, naked and you did not clothe me, sick and in prison and you did not visit me." Then they also will answer, "Lord, when did we see you hungry or thirsty or a stranger or naked or sick or in prison,

and did not minister to you?" Then he will answer them, "Truly, I say to you, as you did it not to one of the least of these, you did it not to me." And they will go away into eternal punishment, but the righteous into eternal life. (Mt 25:31-46)

Here we see the importance of every neighbor, especially those in need. *We* are the ones who need *them* in order to possess eternal life; and if we do not care for them, we cannot escape hell.

Jesus in the needy according to the Fathers of the Church

John Chrysostom tried to open the eyes of the Christians of his day to this truth, which at once inspires fear and joy, and which then, as now, Christians often forgot:

> But we . . . do not even feed [the poor man] when he is hungry. . . . And yet if you saw Christ himself, every one of you would strip himself of all his possessions. But even now it is [Christ], for he himself has said, "It is I." Why then do you not strip yourself of everything? For even now you hear him say, "you do it to me." . . . In fact, if he were not the one to receive what you give, he would not grant you the kingdom. If you were not rejecting [Christ] himself, when you despise him in any person, he would not send you to hell. But it is precisely because you are despising him, that the blame is so great.[1]

Thinking this over carefully, it seems that of all God has commanded us to do, one thing alone is of value: love for the suffering and for those in need. It is "as if," in the words of Leo the Great, "those on the right had no other virtue, and those on the left no other sin."[2]

In reading the Fathers of the Church, I found fiery words that reinforce this truth. The unexcelled master on the subject is the enlightened and forceful John Chrysostom.

The following passage in his *Homilies on the Gospel of Matthew* made my heart jump for joy, because it seems to me that the Lord has always directed us to focus our attention first of all on our neighbor whom we see, in order to love concretely

God whom we do not see—just as the apostle John tells us (cf. 1 Jn 4:20). Then everything else becomes worthwhile, including the liturgy and every form of worship. "So if . . . your brother has something against you, leave your gift there before the altar and go; first be reconciled to your brother" (Mt 5:23-24). "Above all, hold unfailing your love for one another" (1 Pt 4:8).

Here, then, are the eloquent words of John Chrysostom:

> What does Christ gain if his table [altar] is covered with cups of gold, while he himself is dying of hunger in those who are poor? First fill him in his hunger, and then decorate his altar. Will you offer him a golden chalice and not give him a glass of cold water? What good will that do him? You obtain cloths woven with gold for the altar, but you do not offer him the clothes he needs. . . . Tell me: if you were to see a man without sufficient food, would you leave him in his hunger and set about covering the table with silver? Do you think he would thank you, or would he not instead become indignant? And if you were to see someone dressed in rags, and not bother to give him something to wear; but instead, you began to erect gilded columns, saying that you were doing it in his honor, don't you think he would consider that you were mocking him, and that what you were doing was an insult of the worst kind? Then think the same way with regard to Christ when he is going about as a wanderer or a stranger in need of a roof to shelter him. . . . I say this not to prohibit you from honoring him with such gifts, but to exhort you to help the poor as well as give gifts, or rather, to help the poor before giving gifts.
>
> God has never blamed anyone for not having given expensive gifts to adorn his temples; but as regards not helping the poor, he threatens us with hell. Therefore, while adorning his house, do not overlook your brother who is in distress, for he is more properly a temple than the (church building is).
>
> These treasures of yours (in the churches) can be despoiled by unbelieving kings, tyrants, and thieves, but what you have done for your brother who is hungry or a stranger or naked, not even the devil can take from you because it will be laid up in a safe place.[3]

And Cyprian was of the same mind:

With your patrimony ... feed Christ. ... Lay up your treasures where no thief will dig them up and no treacherous robber will break in. Acquire possessions for yourself, but in heaven, where your fruits will last for all eternity, free from every contact with the world's injustice, and where no rust will consume them, where no hail can strike them down, where the sun will not burn them nor the rain ruin them. For you are offending God himself if you believe that he has given you wealth so that you could make use of it without concern for salvation.[4]

Love for the poor becomes a source of great peace and hope when we realize that, since Jesus considers as done to him whatever we do for those in need, he becomes indebted to us and we become his creditors. Ambrose affirms this:

Lend the Lord your money through the hands of the poor. The Lord is held liable; he records whatever the needy man receives. The gospel is your guarantee. ... Why do you hesitate to give? ... For you, the poor man is the Lord of heaven and the Creator of this world. Are you still trying to think how you can find a richer guarantor?[5]

Gifts given to the poor put God under obligation, for it is written, "Whoever gives to the poor lends to the Lord" (Prov 19:17).[6]

And Augustine says that the recompense we will receive from Jesus will be great:

Listen to what you will receive in possessions from him to whom you have made your loan: "Come, O blessed of my Father, inherit. ... " Desire this, work to obtain this, let this be the purpose of your lending.[7]

Jesus in the needy according to the saints

The Curé of Ars once made a statement that shows how the supernatural (and thus true) way of looking at things was almost second nature to him: "Frequently we believe we are giving assistance to a poor person, and in reality it turns out to be the Lord."[8]

On another occasion, he cleared up a doubt that all of us can have when it comes to helping someone unknown:

> There are those who say: "Oh, he will make bad use of it." Let him do what he wants with it. The poor person will be judged on what use he or she made of your gift, and you will be judged on the basis of the gift you could have given and did not give.[9]

The fact is that the saints have always been great experts in loving those who suffer and leaders in establishing all sorts of initiatives and institutions to help them. But above all they have shown themselves to be human beings with hearts. For instance, they say that St. Francis "seemed to have a mother's heart."[10] The saints are persons who have felt the sufferings of the poor and the needy as their own, and have loved Christ in them to such an extent that Our Lord did not wait for the next life in order to show himself to them, as we read of Catherine of Siena:

> She was accosted by a beggar, who asked her, for the love of God, to help him in his need. Not having anything to give him, she told him to wait until she got home. But the beggar persisted: "If you have anything to give me, give it to me now, because the truth is I'm desperate."
>
> Not wishing to send him away disappointed, she wondered what she could give him, and then she remembered a little silver cross that hung at the end of her beads. She quickly broke the thread and gave the beggar the cross. As soon as he had been given it he went off perfectly content without asking anyone else for anything.
>
> During the night, while the virgin of the Lord was as usual at prayer, the Savior of the world appeared to her holding this cross, now adorned with precious stones, in his hand. "Daughter," he said, "do you recognize this cross?" "I certainly do," replied Catherine, "but when it was mine it was not so beautiful." Said the Lord, "I promise you that I will present it to you, just as it is now, in the presence of the angels and men on Judgment Day."
>
> Another day the Lord appeared to her in the likeness of a young

man half-naked. She said to him, "Wait here for me a little while, while I go back into the chapel, and then I will give you clothing." Once inside the chapel, she carefully and modestly pulled down the sleeveless tunic that she wore under her outer tunic and gave it to the poor beggar. He no sooner accepted it than he made another request: "Lady, now that you have supplied me with a woolen garment, will you give me some linen clothes too?" Catherine said, "Follow me." Entering her home, she went into the room where the linen clothes belonging to her father and brothers were kept, took out a shirt and a pair of trousers and with a smile offered them to the beggar. But he said, "Lady, what use is this tunic to me without sleeves?" Whereupon Catherine, not in the least degree put out by this, set off on a careful search of the house. She happened to see the serving woman's dress hanging from a pole, so she quickly unstitched the sleeves, and gave them to the beggar.

He then said, "Look, lady, you have given me a new set of clothing, but I have a friend and he too is in great need of clothing." Catherine remembered that everyone in the house except her father was upset at her continual almsgiving. So she was in two minds as to what to do, whether to give the poor fellow her one remaining piece of clothing or not. Charity suggested she should, but maidenly modesty said no. So she said to the beggar, "If it was lawful for me to go about without a tunic I would give you this one gladly; but I am not allowed to do so." The other replied, "I know you would be very pleased to give me all you could. Farewell."

During the night, while she was praying, there appeared to her the Savior of the world, in the likeness of this beggar, holding in his hand the tunic that Catherine had given him, now decked out with pearls and brilliant gems; and He said to her, "Most beloved daughter, do you recognize this tunic?" When she answered that she did, but that she had not given it to Him in that rich state, the Lord went on, "Yesterday, you clothed me; now I will give you from my holy body a piece of clothing that will certainly be invisible to the eyes of men but which you nevertheless will be able to perceive, and by means of it your soul and body will be protected against all danger of cold until the time comes for you to be clothed with glory and honor in the presence of the saints and the angels." And immediately with His most holy hands He drew forth from the wound in His side a garment the color of blood, and putting it upon her, He said, "I give you this garment with all its powers for the rest of your life on earth, as a sign and token of the garment of glory with which at the appropriate time you will be clothed in heaven." With this the vision vanished.

The holy virgin from that time forward never wore any more clothes in winter than she did in summer.[11]

St. Vincent de Paul's charism of love for the poor and for all those in need continues to shine like a beacon down through the centuries. When he explained their rule to the first Daughters of Charity, he went so far as to say:

> You should know, my daughters, that when you set aside your prayers or the holy Mass in order to serve the poor you will not be losing anything, because serving the poor means going to visit God, and in the poor person you ought to see God.[12]

But let us now look at another great saint of the poor, who made himself poverty for love of Christ. We all know him: Francis of Assisi. He had such a deep sense of universal brotherhood, that he could not conceive of a world with social inequalities, in which some have more and some have less. It is certainly not by chance that he is referred to as the saint most similar to Christ.

> One day when he was riding on horseback through the plain that lies below the town of Assisi, he came upon a leper. This unforeseen encounter struck him with horror. But he recalled his resolution . . . to become a knight of Christ. He . . . ran to kiss the man. When the leper put out his hand as if to receive some alms, Francis gave him money and a kiss. Immediately mounting his horse, Francis looked all around; but although the open plain stretched clear in all directions, he could no longer see the leper anywhere. Filled with wonder and joy, he began to devoutly to sing God's praises . . . [13]

When he met [the poor] he not only generously gave them even the necessities of life that had been given to him, but he believed that these should be given them as if theirs by right. It

110

happened once that a poor man met him . . . when because of an illness [Francis] was wearing a short mantle over his habit. When his kind eye observed the man's misery, he said to his companion: "We should return this mantle to this poor man because it is his. For we got it on loan until we should find someone poorer than ourselves." But his companion, considering the need of his devoted father, obstinately refused, lest Francis provide for another by neglecting himself. But Francis said: "I believe that the great Almsgiver will charge me with theft if I do not give what I have to one who needs it more." Therefore concerning all that was given him to relieve the needs of his body, he was accustomed to ask the permission of the donors to give it away if he should meet someone in greater need. He spared nothing at all, neither mantles, tunics nor books, not even decorations from the altar—all these he gave to the poor when he could.[14]

Jesus in those who suffer, according to Paul VI

Let us now see how Pope Paul VI looked upon those who suffer. His words to the convicts of Rome, when he visited them in 1965, are a sublime affirmation that he saw Jesus in them:

> I love you; not because of some romantic feeling, not because of some compassionate humanitarian impulse, but I truly love you because even now I am discovering in you the image of God, the likeness of Christ. . . .
>
> And now I will tell you . . . a paradox . . . a truth which doesn't seem true. . . . The Lord Jesus . . . has taught us that it is your misfortune, your hurt, your lacerated and faulty humanity which constitutes the very reason for which I have come among you, to love you, to assist you, to console you, and to tell you that you are the image of Christ, that you reproduce the crucified Christ before my eyes. . . . This is why I have come . . . to fall on my knees before you.[15]

On another occasion, speaking about those dedicated to caring for suffering children, he said:

They are destined to be in a sort of perpetual adoration, not of Jesus in his real presence under the Eucharistic species, but of what Bossuet called "the human presence of Jesus Christ in those who suffer."[16]

Paul VI himself explained the presence of Jesus in the poor and the suffering in this way:

> We must remember that Jesus is the Son of Man: it was he who named and defined himself in this way. . . . This means that every human being, every human life, has a connection with him. Jesus is involved in a relationship with every creature, and therefore he has a relationship with everyone who suffers. . . . Jesus draws to himself every human suffering; not only because he is the one who has suffered in the highest degree and as a result of the greatest injustice, but also because . . . he has immense affection and sympathy . . . for those who suffer.[17]

We have now considered some of the aspects of the presence of Jesus in whose who suffer. May we never ever forget that we belong to the Church of the poor, and that the Focolare must therefore be the movement of the poor; all the more so, since this is nothing other than Christianity. At the end of our lives—as we have seen—our final examination will be on this very subject: the so-called "works of mercy." Pope John Paul I said: "The catechism translates this [passage about the Last Judgment in Mt 25:31-46] into the two lists of the works of mercy, seven corporal and seven spiritual."[18]

So let us rectify our intentions, and thereby transform every act of love toward every neighbor in need—whether at home, at work, in school, on the street, or anywhere else—into one of the works of mercy. In this way we will open wide the doors of our hearts to all those we find out about each day who are miserable, abandoned, sick, sinners, alienated, rejected, the dregs of society, or whose human rights are trampled on, whether they are in our own cities and countries or in faraway places.

The poor and the Focolare

Just as we find the poor around the new-born baby Jesus, just as taking care of the poor was one of the main concerns of the early Christian community, just as the saints have often begun their ascent to God by going out to the poor, similarly, around the first signs of life of our movement we find the poor.

I was still living at home on Via Gocciadoro when the first Focolarine and I began this new adventure. I do not know exactly what it was that impelled us to go out with such zeal to the poor of the city of Trent, and to continue this zealous activity later on in the first focolare center. I think it must have been the words of Jesus, "Whatever you did to the least you did to me" (cf. Mt 25:40).

I remember the rather long corridor of my house filled with anything that could be of use to the poor: cases of jam, cans of powdered milk, sacks of flour, clothes, medicine, and firewood.

I remember that we had very little time, because all of us were working or going to school. So at lunch time, as soon as we had finished eating, we would set out for the three poorest neighborhoods in the city: Androne, Laste, and Portella. Each of us carried two packed and heavy suitcases. It was always a race!

It meant climbing dark flights of stairs, old and dangerous, eaten away by time and vermin, into almost total darkness, into desolate situations which pained our young hearts. Having mounted the stairs, we would find a room without light, its poor occupant in bed, generally lacking everything. It was Jesus. We would wash and console him or her, make promises in the name of the almighty God, and give whatever we could.

On one occasion, a Focolarina was loving Jesus in a poor woman with all her heart. She remained in the woman's house for some time, giving it a thorough cleaning, and finally sang her a song dedicated to mothers. Afterward, this Focolarina found she had caught an infection which produced open sores all over her face. But immediately she was happy because she was able to be a little bit similar to Jesus forsaken.

113

Whenever a poor person would come to our homes, we would choose the best tablecloth, the best dishes and tableware. Frequently what we gave him or her to eat consisted of what we had deprived ourselves of at lunch or dinner, by slipping our bread, cheese or whatever under the table when our parents were not looking, and involving our little sisters in the game as well.

When we went out each of us carried a pocket notebook, and our hearts would jump for joy whenever we met poor persons. We would approach them with great love and ask for their names and addresses so that we would be able to love, as we would say, "to the end."

Yes, for although our immediate concern was certainly to help each individual poor person, from the start we did so with a very precise plan in mind: we wanted to resolve the social problem of the city of Trent. God did not let us see anything else, almost as if, once it were accomplished, all the world's problems would have been solved. And so we focused our efforts on those who lived in the destitute areas of the city, in order to alleviate their condition: first, by providing them with medicine, food, and wood for heat; and, later on, by finding jobs for them.

Quite often episodes occurred in which it was evident that God had intervened to encourage us, and some of these are still recounted today.

In the first focolare center on Piazza Cappuccini the work continued just as intensely. Each day we would make a huge pot of soup which we would then take to the poor in a neighborhood called San Martino. But the poor people also regarded the Focolare as their home, and they would come and eat with us; and at table there would be a poor person, then a Focolarina, a poor person, a Focolarina, and so on.

Then the war ended, and the poor became better off; and gradually we began to disperse throughout Italy to announce the Gospel we had rediscovered.

But wherever the Focolare has since spread throughout the world, whenever there has been a need, as in the Cameroons or Brazil, or parts of Asia; or whenever the Gen (the "New Generation" of the Focolare movement) have repeated the experience of the first generation, whether the context was similar or not, the poor have always been with us.

Moreover, the Focolare as a whole is now experiencing a new springtime as regards going out to assist others, through the New Humanity Movement, which is animated by members of the Focolare and guided by its spirit. This New Humanity Movement has timidly but decisively put itself at the service of society, particularly today's poor: the drug addicts, the alienated, the unemployed, the sinners, the amoral, the unbelievers.

"Die for our people" is the motto of this operation which re-echoes and relives what Jesus did.

In this way we live and work, awaiting the day when Jesus can say to all of us: I was an outsider and you brought me into your community, I was on drugs and you gave me back true happiness, I was unemployed and you found me a job. I had no standards to live by, and you taught me God's law. I was without God, and you made me rediscover him as Love, by drawing me into your own divine adventure.

CHRIST AND THE NON-CHRISTIANS

Christians and the faithful of other religions

The Focolare's experience

For some time now, due to its expansion throughout the world, the Focolare has been coming into contact with many members of non-Christian faiths, even though it has only recently begun giving this immense number of believers very special attention.

Our attitude toward these non-Christians brothers and sisters has been to love them. And love itself has been a source of light, enabling us to know how to approach them.

Love, which induces Christians to be the first to love, prompted us to take an interest in everything that concerns them: from their worries about their families, work, school, and social condition, to their spiritual concerns and so on, all the way up to their religious beliefs.

Christian love may seem like mere human friendship, but if it is prompted by supernatural motives it causes us not only to give to others but to confide in them, to give what we have and what we are. And so, these brothers and sisters of ours have come to know everything about us, from the little things to our great ideal: Christ, who has taken first place in our lives.

This was possible, still is, and always will be, because with love as our starting point, we have found glimmers of Gospel truth in their religious thought. And in their lives we have found acts full of sacrifice and love for others, along with principles which are sound and universally acceptable. On this basis we are able to make a serene and peaceful comparison between their faith and ours, between their life and the Christian life.

This results in an indirect evangelization of these brothers and sisters, who accept dialogue based on love and life, and subsequently also accept dialogue on matters of faith. At the same time it provokes a common desire to take seriously those elements which already unite us and to live them, in order to work together to make the world better through religion. As a result, they are not reluctant to unite themselves to our movement, participating in our meetings and in the life of the Focolare's various branches, as Muslim or Buddhist Gen or Volunteers, Buddhist or Hindu monks or nuns, and so on.

This has been our small experience, which is still continuing and which we hope will take on ever larger dimensions in the future.

Vatican II and the non-Christian religions[1]

Let us now look at what the Church—and in particular Vatican II—teaches about the faithful of other religions and about the relationships that Christians should have with them. We will avail ourselves of the Council documents so that our own work may have a broader approach, greater depth and a stronger foundation.

The Council acknowledged that "the Holy Spirit was already at work in the world before Christ was glorified,"[2] and believed that the same Holy Spirit is also at work today among non-Christians. Therefore, "the Catholic Church rejects nothing which is true and holy in these religions."[3]

The Council recognized that numerous elements of truth and grace are to be found among the non-Christians, as a sort of hidden presence of God,[4] and acknowledged that their religions "often reflect a ray of that truth which enlightens all men."[5] Moreover, it speaks of "the seeds of the Word which lie hidden in them [the non-Christians]."[6]

Justin, a second-century philosopher and martyr, held that the divine Word (*Logos*) is wholly present only in Jesus, but that, given the instrumental role of the Word in creation, "seeds of the Word"[7] have been sown throughout the whole of humanity, so that in every human being there is a seed of the Word.

117

The *Decree on the Church's Missionary Activity* also recognizes "the ascetic and contemplative traditions whose seeds were sometimes already planted by God in ancient cultures prior to the preaching of the gospel."[8] Moreover, it says that all these spiritual and religious values, which are found both in the individual non-Christians and in their rites and cultures, "through the kindly workings of Divine Providence, may sometimes serve as a guidance course toward the true God, or as a preparation for the gospel."[9]

However, since "rather often men, deceived by the Evil One, have become caught up in futile reasoning and have exchanged the truth of God for a lie, serving the creature rather than the Creator,"[10] they need the Church's presence. For "[the Church's missionary] activity frees from all taint of evil and restores to Christ its maker whatever truth and grace are to be found among the nations."[11]

This means that the behavior of individual Christians as well, must be characterized by prudence and discernment.[12]

How Christians should act toward members of other religions[13]

Vatican II lays great stress on how Christians should behave toward non-Christians. It encourages them to "gladly and reverently" uncover "the seeds of the Word which lie hidden in them [the non-Christians]." And it goes on to say:

> Christians should know the people among whom they live, and should establish contact with them. Thus they themselves can learn by sincere and patient dialogue what treasures a bountiful God has distributed among the nations of the earth. But at the same time, let them try to illumine these treasures with the light of the gospel.[14]

The Council also urges that the exposition of the Word of God be adapted to the customs, culture, and mentality of the various peoples, and that "theological investigation" be fostered, avoiding, of course, "every appearance of syncretism and of false particularism."[15]

Anything in their way of life that is not indissolubly bound up with superstition and error she [the Church] studies with sympathy and, if possible, preserves intact. Sometimes in fact she admits such things into the liturgy itself.[16]

And finally, the Council invites all Christians to work together with non-Christians for peace, justice, freedom, and religion.[17] And in the *Dogmatic Constitution on the Church*, it makes the following very clear affirmation:

Those who have not yet received the gospel are related in various ways to the People of God. In the first place there is the people to whom the Covenants and the promises were given and from whom Christ was born according to the flesh. . . .
But the plan of salvation also includes those who acknowledge the Creator. In the first place among these are the Muslims. . . . Nor is God Himself far distant from those who in shadows and images seek the unknown God, for it is He who gives to all men life . . . and who as Savior wills that all men be saved (cf. 1 Tim 2:4).[18]

The human person as viewed by the great religions

Let us now—though in a necessarily limited way—consider some of the more prominent non-Christian religions, and see what importance they give to one's neighbor—or better, to human beings as such.

The Judaic tradition

I will not pause now to further consider the Judaic view of the human person, since we have already taken a look at what the Old Testament has to say on the subject, and we have seen that love of neighbor is one of its central norms.

It is unnecessary to say that for us Christians, the Jews are our closest brothers and sisters, because of the immense divine truths which we have in common and which bind us together. It is logical to think that one of these days Jesus will illuminate these blood relatives of his with the full light of the truth, because it is impossible for him not to love them in a very special way, after all the extraordinary graces that God has poured out on them as his chosen people.

The Islamic tradition

Let us move on to Islam.

The Islamic faith is founded upon witness: "There is no God but Allah (the God); and Muhammad is the Messenger of Allah." This is the formula for the profession of faith which incorporates one into Islam and makes one a "believer" and, after death, a "guest of paradise."

This faith is a gift of God. It demands first of all the witness and the adherence of the heart, which renders one "a believer in the eyes of God." It also demands a spoken witness, which makes one "a believer in the eyes of men." And finally it demands that witness be given by carrying out the works prescribed by the Law.

The precepts of the divine Law are found in the Koran (which contains God's revelations to Muhammad). They govern religious practices and lay down norms for all human activity. The principal religious observances prescribed are known traditionally as "the Pillars of Islam" and are: the proclamation of the profession of faith (given above); ritual prayer to be performed five times a day; almsgiving according to the Law; fasting during the month of Ramadan; pilgrimage to Mecca at least once during one's lifetime. There are numerous other precepts which include instructions regarding food, funerals, visits to cemeteries, marriage and family life, and relationships in society.

Even though the witness of faith saves one directly ("those whose heart contains an atom of faith will escape hell"), in large areas of the Muslim world today it seems that faith without works, without some moral and civil commitment, is less and less acceptable. For a sincere Muslim today, "good works" are often more important than an external observance of the Pillars of Islam. Moreover, many passages in the Koran stress the duty to help one's neighbor; to come to the assistance of orphans, the poor, the unhappy; to keep one's word; to welcome travelers; to ransom prisoners; and so on.[19]

In Islam as well, therefore, one's neighbor is given some consideration.

Muslim customs, which are based on the *aklaq*, are also strict. And in the Koran, frequent passages on how to behave toward one's neighbor call to mind the content of the commandments in Exodus and Deuteronomy.

> You shall show kindness to your parents; you shall not kill your children because you cannot support them (We provide for you and for them); you shall not commit foul sins, whether openly or in secret; and you shall not kill—for that is forbidden by Allah—except for a just cause (Koran 6:151).
>
> Allah enjoins justice, kindness and charity to one's kindred (Koran 16:90).[20]

Moreover, the Koran condemns adultery, fornication, homosexuality, stealing, and giving false testimony.

Muslim morality, therefore, is based on God. But in spite of the value given to works, good or bad actions which do not directly involve faith still have only relative importance when compared to giving witness to the one God and to his Messenger.[21]

Islam is a religion, but it is also inseparably community, culture, and civilization. However, it is not a "state" in the modern juridical sense of the term. The "community of believers" may coincide with a single empire, as it did in earlier times, or with a multitude of sultanates, kingdoms, and republics, as it does today.

As members of the "community of the Prophet," Muslims feel that they are "believers" and that they are "entrusted to God." And in the community they find strength, peace, and the full development of their human dignity.[22]

Among the strongest sociological realities of the Muslim world is brotherhood. The Koran says: "Remember the favors

He has bestowed upon you: how He united your hearts when you were enemies, so that you are now brothers through His grace" (Koran 3:103).

However, this brotherhood is only open to those who wish to embrace Islam, and equality among all men takes effect only after their conversion. Even so, Islam's attitude toward the "People of the Book" (Jews and Christians) is different from its attitude toward pagans.

For although the Koran recognizes the obligation to show hospitality and to give to those in need, it is severe toward pagans, who are considered enemies: "Muhammad is Allah's apostle. Those who follow him are ruthless to the unbelievers [polytheists] but merciful to one another" (Koran 48:29).

In Islam one does not go to God by means of loving one's neighbor, nor is God to be found in our fellow human beings, nor does faith lose any of its value if there is no fraternal love. Kindness toward one's neighbor—or, better, toward one's fellow Muslim—can, at most, bring one to faith in God, but in just the same way as would any of the other "good works" or religious practices. Such benevolent love, by virtue of the fact that it unites people, is a preparation for the revelation of the unity of God.[23]

For this reason, those Focolarini who have been in contact with Muslims affirm that the way to present our religion to these brothers and sisters is to live in perfect unity among ourselves, in a unity that is stronger than theirs because of the presence of Christ in our midst (cf. Mt 18:20).

Our belief in the Trinity of God arouses reservations and misunderstandings among Muslims because they fear that it is against the unity of God. But this strong unity among us, since it gives witness to the unity of God, makes them think of the one and only God who is at the heart of their faith, and in whom we also believe.

Hindu perspectives

Hinduism is the result of the history of a people which has dedicated its finest energies to the pursuit of the spiritual. The fixed point in this quest, the milestone to which reference is always made is the intuition that Reality is One.

The gods, humans, the world, all the things that have been, are, or ever will be: all this is one and the same Reality: "The whole universe is Brahman" (*Chandogya Upanishad* III, 14, 1). And when a person has reached the state of enlightenment, he or she may also say: "I am Brahman" (*Brihadaranyaka Upanishad* I, 4, 10). Brahman is "one only—without a second" (*Chandogya Upanishad* VI, 2, 1-3).

The innermost self—Atman—of a person is also identical with Brahman:

> He is my Self within the heart, smaller than a grain of rice or a barley corn, or a mustard seed, or a grain of millet; this is my Self within my heart, greater than the earth, greater than the atmosphere, greater than the sky. . . . This my Self within the heart is that Brahman. (*Chandogya Upanishad* III, 14, 3-4).

And as far as the individual is concerned, for centuries Hinduism has been repeating the phrase of Uddalaka to his son Svetaketu: "That [Brahman-Atman] *you* are!" (*Chandogya Upanishad* VI 8, 7; 10, 3; 11, 3; 13, 3; 14, 3; 15, 3; 16, 2).

In this way the Brahman-Atman is recognized as the sole Absolute, the root and foundation of everything, the Lord who upholds and sustains all things, the inner guide and the goal of every living thing. . . .

Everything that is apparent is the selfsame Brahman who manifests himself through each thing. He is the true Reality of every one of his manifestations. Only if a phenomenon is considered on its own can we speak of beginning or end, of birth or death; but the phenomenon itself has always been in the bosom of Brahman, and will be conserved in Him eternally.

Not only does one not die, but in reality one has never been born.

> Never was there a time when I was not, nor you, nor yet these lords of men; nor will there be a time when we shall cease to

be—all of us hereafter. Just as in this body the embodied soul must pass through childhood, youth and age, so too at death will he take another body up. (*Bhagavad-Gita* II, 12-13)

So the deepest Self of every human being, the true Person, is the Atman and that is identical to Brahman:

Indestructible, eternal, unborn, never to pass away. . . . As a man casts off his worn-out clothes and takes on other new ones, so does the embodied soul cast off his worn-out bodies and enters others new. (*Bhagavad-Gita* II, 20-25)[24]

Therefore, in the words of P. Rossano:

In the monistic view of Hinduism, earthly reality actually disappears: "It is not for the love of a husband that a husband is dearly loved. Rather it is for love of the Self [Atman] that a husband is dearly loved. . . . It is not for the love of a wife that a wife is dearly loved. Rather it is for love of the Self [Atman] that a wife is dearly loved. . . . It is not for love of [anything] that [anything] is dearly loved. Rather it is for love of the Self [Atman] that [anything] is dearly loved" (*Brihadaranyaka Upanishad* II, 4, 5). Nothing is loved for its own sake, but always for love of Atman. The Atman is all that is.[25]

One can understand, then, the words of another author:

Love of the neighbor as such is scarcely ever directly enjoined in the Hindu Scriptures, and one would search in vain for anything like the "new commandment" of the Gospel. . . . According to the *Isa Upanishad*, he who sees all things in the Self (Atman) and the Self in all things, does not shrink back or run away from anything. It is impossible for him to esteem more highly the "manifestation" of the Atman, the unique Self, in his own body and mind than the "manifestation" of the same unique Self in the body and mind of anyone else. In the light of that Self he cannot experience, or even think of, himself as separate from others. His awareness of himself as a particular thinking and perceiving individual is completely shot through with the awareness of the Self as unparticularized and unconditioned. He truly loves "himself" in every being.[26]

And is thus liberated from all egoism.

> But whatever might be the practical consequences of this formulation of Hindu wisdom [such as frequent indifference toward the physical and spiritual needs of one's neighbor], the real *jnani* [wise man] loves uniquely well, and all who have met such a *jnani* will testify to this fact. No matter what philosophy he employs to express his outlook, the *jnani's* actions, the look in his eyes, and his consideration for each individual, all speak eloquently of the love that fills his heart. He is entirely transparent to the Spirit, and there is nothing in him to obstruct the moving of the Spirit; from his heart the Spirit flows forth to every heart. . . . He is all things to all men, to every man. For himself he demands and expects nothing, since all that comes to him passes through him to the Lord himself within him.[27]

God is living in these non-Christian contemplatives and manifesting himself—unknown to them—for what he is: Love.

Toward the third century B.C., alongside the absolute monism of Hinduism, a new and flourishing doctrine appeared: Bhakti, centered on God's love for the human person and human love for God.[28] Whereas Brahman is impersonal, in Bhakti God is also personal. Moreover, the external world and individual souls are not lost in the divinity, but seem to possess a consistency of their own. In Bhakti, which means "devotion," "love," the human being is engaged in a "loving, trusting flight toward God."[29]

All this must stimulate us Christians to live up to the Gospel with all its demands—since it is the revelation of God who is Love—so that there will not be just a few saints who give witness to God, but a great part of Christendom will give witness to him.

Then many of those young people who in their search for the spiritual are investigating the ways of India will find among the followers of Christ the ideal they are looking for.

Buddhist perspectives

Buddhism was initially a purely ethical doctrine, which through the centuries has developed into various religious sects and philosophical schools.

The intention of Buddha ("the Enlightened One"), after his personal experience, was only to show others the way to reach freedom from suffering and from endless reincarnation. Reincarnation—inherited from Hinduism—is considered an undisputed truth in Buddhism.

For Buddha, everything in the world is suffering and sorrow, because everything is transitory. The human person is also composed of psycho-physical elements which are continually changing with no permanent or unchanging principle—therefore with no soul.

Buddha taught that the source of suffering is desire, whatever form this desire may take, because everything that one desires to have or to be is only transitory.

In order to extinguish suffering, therefore, one must suppress all desires, eradicate passions and selfishness, subdue every affirmation of one's ego. In this way—while still in this life, and even more so after one's physical death—through one's own efforts one may reach "Nirvana," the state of complete freedom from all desire, of the absolute absence of suffering, of indescribable peace, in which the painful cycle of reincarnation is broken.

One can only reach this state gradually through the practice of the Eightfold Path of the Buddhist ethic. Detachment from everything is a requirement for everyone. However, this is only carried out completely in the monastic life, in which one "seeks refuge" not only "in Buddha" and "in the Law," but also "in the community" as such.[30] For in the community, one finds the best conditions for reaching that full illumination which allows one to intuit the true nature of things—which is their "emptiness"— and in this way to extinguish all desire.

Regarding relationship with one's neighbor, Buddhism stresses the practice of virtue, particularly benevolence and unselfish love, in order to purify the heart of attachments. But it does not consider love as the way to human perfection nor as an integral part of it.

Through the centuries, Buddhism has split into two main currents or schools. Mahayana (the "greater vehicle"), more open to the people, has introduced a greater concern for others into the earlier doctrine of Theravada Buddhism (the "way of the elders").

The innovations of Mahayana Buddhism derive from a new definition of the Buddha and a new conception of humanity. Buddha is "Nothingness," "Emptiness"—not an emptiness of being, but the absence of every dialectic and of every human category. He transcends them. He is the Absolute itself (*solutus ab:* "freed from"). He is infinite light, infinite life, infinite mercy. "The Buddha is love" (*Kan-mu-ryo-ju-kyo*), "he is the infinite love which pardons all" (*Mahaprajnaparamita-sutra*, 27). He is "the Father and the Savior of all creatures" (*Saddharmapundarika-sutra*, 18). And "every person potentially possesses the nature of Buddha" (*Mahaparinirvana-sutra*, 27). Therefore, to Mahayana Buddhists, denying oneself is the indispensable condition for activating this potential, for allowing Buddha to live in them.[31]

> From the new vision of Buddha and of human nature comes also the need to love one's neighbor. . . . The apex of Mahayana asceticism consists of seeing Buddha in everyone and everyone in Buddha. . . . Particularly significant in this regard is the following allegory: "Imagine a thousand watery surfaces: that of a large river or of a large lake, of a clear fountain or of a dirty puddle. All of them reflect the moon. The moon reflected on one of these thousand surfaces is not the thousandth part of the moon, but the one and entire moon. One sees a thousand moons, but in reality there is only one moon in the sky. As there are a thousand reflections of the same moon, so men are many reflections of the same Buddha: small or great, miserable or holy—this does not matter. The moon reflected is always the whole moon. Buddha also is always entire in men" (Inscription of Hsin-hsin-ming).

According to Mahayana doctrine, every person is a *bodhisattva*; that is, a being destined for enlightenment. In order to reach this enlightenment he takes a vow to become Buddha, he asks his help and commits himself to the serious practice of these virtues: "generosity toward all, morality in living, patience even toward enemies, vigor, contemplation, and wisdom."

All the actions of the *bodhisattva* must be motivated by love toward all creatures. "To serve creatures is to serve Buddha, is to fulfill my purpose, is to eliminate the world's suffering" (*Bodhicaryavatara*, VI, 127).

The *bodhisattva* . . . works untiringly for the salvation of all creatures, without ever desiring to enter Nirvana until he has saved all the others:

> The compassionate man [the *bodhisattva*], who with the strength of wisdom has uprooted all self-love, because of his love for all creatures never withdraws into Peace [Nirvana] (*Ratnagotra-vibha-sastra*, 35).

Therefore, the Mahayana Buddhist wishes to remain in the world of reincarnation for the total Buddhafication of the universe. This is Mahayanan salvation: "Whoever does not save the others does not save even himself" (*Mu-chu-mon-do-shu*, 49).[32]

In short, the older Theravada Buddhism seeks self-liberation from suffering and relies only on human efforts. Mahayana Buddhism, on the other hand, teaches trust in the help that can come from above and a great openness toward others.

Christ and nonbelievers

We have taken a rapid look at what sort of consideration the major religions give to the human person.

Now let us see what relationship exists between Christ and members of non-Christian religions as well as nonbelievers.

Jesus said that his earthly mission concerned Israel (cf. Mt 15:24), but his thinking and his behavior were stupendously open. He offered a Samaritan to the Jews as a model. He stated that "he that is not against us is for us" (Mk 9:40), even if the person is not one of his disciples. He admired the faith of the centurion and of the Canaanite woman: they are signs and preludes of the fact that "men will come from the east and the west, and from north and south, and sit at table in the kingdom of God" (Lk 13:29). He asks for love of enemies, and he cares for the sinner and those who suffer, no matter who they are.

We must also take another look at the scene of the Last Judgment (Mt 25:31-46), included in the preceding chapter, especially Jesus' words: "As you did it to one of the least of these my brethren, you did it to me." According to the majority of Scripture scholars, the phrase "the least of these brethren" refers to anyone in need, whether Christian or non-Christian. In fact, the context in which Jesus says these words is universal. He has before him "all the nations"—that is, all peoples, without restriction (see also Mt 28:19).

In this text the evangelist's intention is certainly not to describe in detail how the Final Judgment will be carried out, but to tell us that love is the criterion on which everyone will be judged. In fact, each person who performs concrete acts of love will receive the kingdom as an inheritance: he or she will be saved. Therefore, every person who loves, whether aware of it or not, enters into direct contact with Christ, into a relationship with him, and is his brother or sister.

Therefore, every person who loves is acting under the influence of grace. As the Council states:

> Since Christ died for all men, and since the ultimate vocation of man is in fact one, and divine, we ought to believe that the Holy Spirit in a manner known only to God offers to every man the possibility of being associated with this paschal mystery.[33]

Salvation, therefore, is for "all men of good will," that is for those who respond to the secret call of their hearts, in which "grace works in an unseen way."[34]

The ways by which non-Christians and nonbelievers are saved [35]

The Council brings out the fact that non-Christians, even nonbelievers, can come to the knowledge of God and attain salvation through created things and through following their own conscience.

The *Dogmatic Constitution on Divine Revelation*, states that "God, who through the Word creates all things and keeps them in existence, gives men an enduring witness to Himself in created realities."[36]

And the *Pastoral Constitution on the Church in the Modern World* declares:

> Conscience is the most secret core and sanctuary of a man. There he is alone with God, whose voice echoes in his depths. In a wonderful manner conscience reveals that law which is fulfilled by love of God and neighbor (cf. Mt 22:37-40; Gal 5:14).[37]

There is no doubt that the Council considers that love for God, even if he is imperfectly known, and love of neighbor, when it is demonstrated by actions, are useful ways that "help men to attain to salvation."[38]

Moreover, the Council sees the Spirit of God at work in the progress of the social order which aims at promoting the welfare of the human person.[39] And it also sees his active presence in the area of scientific research: "Indeed, whoever labors to penetrate the secrets of reality with a humble and steady mind, is, even unaware, being led by the hand of God."[40]

Furthermore, the *Dogmatic Constitution on the Church* says:

> Nor does divine Providence deny the help necessary for salvation to those who, without blame on their part, have not yet arrived at an explicit knowledge of God, but who strive to live a good life, thanks to His grace. Whatever goodness or truth is found among them is looked upon by the Church as a preparation for the gospel.[41]

Christians and non-Christians

In his Gospel, John affirms: "He who does what is true comes to the light, that it may be clearly seen that his deeds have been brought in God" (2:31). Therefore, the person "who does what is true" (that is, what is good) is already "in God," in a certain communion with him. And this is clear.

To be "in God," however, is the foundation; it is not yet full communion with him. This full communion comes about only in the encounter with Christ. In a recent ecumenical translation of the Bible we find this comment: "The one who does what is good is already in a certain communion with God and is tending toward the full encounter which takes place in his Son."[42]

The Father brings all those who belong to him to Christ (cf. Jn 17:6). Indeed, he is at work deep within each person's life—while fully respecting his or her freedom—preparing each one to meet Jesus: "no one can come to me unless the Father who sent me draws him. . . . Everyone who has heard and learned from the Father comes to me" (Jn 6:44-45).

The full encounter with Jesus demands a new birth, which only the Spirit can bring about (as we have seen in speaking of the presence of Jesus in the Christian). Then, according to Paul, the person becomes a "new creation" in Christ (2 Cor 5:17). He or she is renewed in the depths of his or her being (cf. 2 Cor 4:16). The acceptance of the Gospel—the encounter with Jesus—transforms a person. It truly makes of him or her a new being; it unites him or her ontologically and vitally to the risen Christ. This is what constitutes the "newness of life" (Rom 6:4) in which the Christian lives.

The task of the Church

At times non-Christians are referred to as being "Christians implicitly," or as "anonymous Christians," or as "Christians who don't know they are Christians." But this does not mean that the only difference between them and Christians lies in knowing or not knowing that one is a Christian. Nor is the work of the Church merely aimed at rendering explicit a reality which persons of good will might already possess.

The Council states that Christ, through his Spirit,

> had established His body, the Church, as the universal sacrament of salvation. . . . He is continually active in the world, leading men to the Church, and through her joining them more closely to Himself.[43]

And in himself, he unites them to the Father and to one another.

This explains the active role of the Church and, above all, its task to "preach the gospel to the whole creation" (Mk 16:15).

Every person on earth, if he or she is "of good will," is a candidate for heaven. This means that even as it strives toward the day "that they may all be one" (Jn 17:21), the Church already embraces, in one way or another, all the good that exists in the world.

HOW TO LOVE OUR NEIGHBOR

The path to reach God

God gives each one who seeks him a way to find him. And often each person is convinced that his or her way is the shortest route to reach him.

I suppose no one could have made St. Teresa of Avila doubt that she had discovered the fastest way to get to God. She says that if you want to find God, you had better look for him where he is: in the center of your heart.

St. Francis finds God through nature as well. His "Canticle of the Sun," which is intended to embrace the whole universe, reveals his concept of God: he is Creator and Father of all that exists. Therefore, animals and flowers, the sun, the moon and the stars, and men and women are all brothers and sisters.

It would be beautiful if we could get to know one by one the ways that God has opened up for people to reach him; this is what the followers of the various saints have always tried to do.

But let us consider our own case. Those familiar with the Focolare know that when God called me to consecrate myself to him forever, the fascination of that call and the elation which flooded my whole being because I had married God were so unique and exceptional that I would have never ever wanted anyone or anything to break the enchantment of the one-to-one relationship with him. If they had told me that day that I was going to have companions, if they had revealed to me that a movement was going to be born, I feel that something divine and inexpressible would have been broken.

But God very quickly made it clear to me, as only he knows how, that loving him involved doing something specific: loving him in my brothers and sisters, in every brother and sister in the world.

God's conception of human nature is something un-imaginable! In 1949, I wrote:

> The Father, Jesus, Mary, us. The Father permitted Jesus to feel forsaken by him *for us*. Jesus accepted being forsaken by the Father and he deprived himself of his Mother *for us*. Mary shared Jesus' abandonment and accepted the loss of her Son *for us*. Therefore *we* are put in first place. It is love which does such crazy things. So we too, when God's will requires it, must leave the Father, Jesus, and Mary for our brother or sister.

Thus our neighbor took a definite place in our heart.

But "the one who loses finds" (cf. Mt 10:39), and immediately it became clear to us that our neighbor was not to be loved merely for his or her own sake, but rather we had to love Christ in him or her. Jesus had said: "as you did it to one of the least of these my brethren [which includes everyone], you did it to me" (Mt 25:40). Consequently, our whole previous way of looking at people and of loving them collapsed. If in some way Christ was in everyone, we could not practice discrimination or have preferences. Out went all the human criteria by which persons are classified as countrymen or alien, old or young, beautiful or ugly, pleasant or unpleasant, rich or poor. Christ was behind each person; Christ was in each person. Every neighbor was truly another Christ if his or her soul was enriched with God's grace; and even if someone was without grace, he or she was still potentially another Christ.

Living in this manner we came to the realization that our neighbor was our way to God. Each brother or sister appeared to us as a doorway through which we had to pass in order to encounter God.

We experienced this right from the very first days. After having loved God all day in our brothers and sisters, in the evening, in recollection or in prayer, we would experience a wonderful union with him. Who could have given us that consolation, that inner peace, so new and heavenly, if not Christ who was living the words of his Gospel: "Give, and it will be given to you" (Lk 6:38)? We had loved him all day in our neighbors, and now he was loving us.

These interior gifts were of great benefit to us. They were our first experiences of the spiritual life, of the reality of a kingdom which is not of this world. And so the Focolare was able to begin its march through the world which does not belong to Christ, because our hearts had experienced that love which is not of the world.

The bond between love of God and love of neighbor

Our experience, therefore, tells us this: love of neighbor comes from love of God; but love for God blossoms in our hearts because we love our neighbor.

It was a comfort for me to find this same experience in Catherine of Siena. In her *Dialogue* she writes that the Eternal Father instructed her with these words:

> Now I want to speak to you about the second mistake made by those who find all their delight in seeking spiritual consolation. . . . If these people are unable to have their consolations, they think they are committing sin; and instead . . . they do not see that they offend me more by not meeting the needs of our neighbor. . . .
> Since they do not help their neighbor, fraternal love diminishes in them; and when this love diminishes, so does my affection toward them. And when my affection for them diminishes, the consolations diminish as well.[1]

We have known from the very beginning of the Focolare that there was a bond between love of God and love of neighbor. Igino Giordani* used to explain our way with this threefold expression: I—my neighbor—God.

---

* *Igino Giordani is a well-known writer, journalist, and university professor. He has also been a member of the Italian Parliament. In 1949, he became the first married Focolarino.*

Gregory the Great speaks masterfully about the relationship between love of God and love of neighbor, using an example which is also very familiar to us: the root and the plant.

> There are two precepts regarding Charity: love of God and love of neighbor. Love of neighbor is born of love of God, and love of God is nourished by love of neighbor. For whoever neglects to love God, is quite incapable of love of neighbor. And we can advance more perfectly in love of God, if first, in the bosom of his love, we are nursed with the milk of love of neighbor. Since love of God generates love of neighbor, in giving the Law, the Lord first set down, "You shall love the Lord our God" (Dt 6:5), before he said, "You shall love your neighbor" (Mt 22:39). Thus, in the soil of our hearts he first planted the root of love toward him, and then, like foliage, fraternal love developed. And that the love of God is bound to love of neighbor is also attested to by John, when he says: "He who does not love his brother whom he has seen, cannot love God whom he has not seen" (1 Jn 4:20).[2]

Isidore of Seville emphasized that "Charity consists in love of God and neighbor. . . . Whoever separates himself from fraternal communion is deprived of a share in God's love."[3] And the Curé of Ars warned: "Never lose sight of the fact that all the time you are not loving your neighbor, the good God is furious with you."[4]

St. John of the Cross makes the following affirmation:

> When one's love for a creature is purely spiritual and founded in God alone, then in the measure that it grows, love for God grows in one's soul as well. Then, the more the heart is aware of the neighbor, the more it is also aware of God and desires him, the two loves vying to outdo each other as they grow.[5]

Therese of Lisieux copied the above words on the back of a holy picture for a novice who feared that she loved her novice mistress too much.

Edouard Dhanis beautifully portrays the love of neighbor as an "overflowing" of one's love for God onto one's fellow human beings. Our movement thinks the same way.

If one asks what is the way in which Jesus envisions the close union between fraternal love and love for God, we must answer that he views the first as an overflowing of the second. He wanted his disciples to put their hearts in unison with the heart of the heavenly Father—if I may use this expression—so that their love for God would extend to all those whom he loves as his children. . . . St. John indicated this with the following expression, rich in meaning: "Every one who loves the parent [God] loves the child [one's fellow human being]."

And he goes on to say:

One of the deeply comforting features in the countenance of the Church today—in the midst of the crisis which is shaking her . . . is a sort of renewed understanding in many of the faithful of the primacy owed to the love of God and neighbor in the Christian life. This renewal is apparent in exegesis, and in moral and spiritual theology. I am referring to a reality that is intensely lived in some religious institutes and movements in which there is a full awareness that authentic Christian love cannot be lived without the cross of Jesus, but where—for this very reason—there reigns a joy which makes one think of heaven.[6]

The author notes that in so writing he had in mind the Little Brothers of Foucauld and the Focolare.

In an editorial in *La Civiltà Cattolica*, among other things, the writer tries to shed light on both the distinction and the bond between the two commandments: love God and love your neighbor. Love for God and love for one's neighbor, we are told, "were known to Jesus' contemporaries, because they are found in the Old Testament (Dt 6:5; Lv 19:18)."

What is characteristic about Jesus is the great emphasis he gives to these two commandments over all the others, and the bond he puts between them, making them into one double-faceted commandment and placing the foundation for love of neighbor in one's love for God.

Jesus gives pre-eminence to love for God. . . . He must be loved with absolute totality: that is, "with all your heart, with all your soul, and with all your mind" (Mt 22:37). . . .

Jesus' love for his fellow human beings and his willingness to sacrifice himself for them spring from his love for the Father. In fact, as he is about to face his passion and death he says: "But the world must know that I love the Father and do as the Father has commanded me. Come then, let us go" (Jn 14:31).[7]

It is Christ in us who must love our neighbor.

To love our neighbor, every neighbor, as the Holy Spirit taught us to do at the beginning of the Focolare, was an authentic revolution. At that time, the Christians whom we knew who were seeking the way to perfection tended to view their neighbor as an obstacle to their reaching God. They based their approach on spiritualities which were good, excellent, but which were primarily suited to those who were called to abandon the world and live in a monastery or convent. And so, at times, they deformed these spiritualities.

How could we have fled from other people, when we were called to live among them? The Lord used a special technique to teach us to love our neighbor, remaining in the world without being of the world. He immediately made us understand that it was possible for us to love our neighbor without falling into sentimentalism or other errors, because he himself could love in us, with his love: charity. We were loving Christ in the other person, but it was also Christ in us who had to love.

And what is charity? As we know, it is a love which comes from above. Paul says "God's love has been poured into our hearts through the Holy Spirit which has been given to us" (Rom 5:5). Charity, therefore, is a sharing in the divine *agape* (love). This charity, this love, is spontaneous, always new; it continually finds different ways to express itself. It does not allow itself to be categorized. It invents unforeseeable solutions. Consequently, Paul tells us: "Be guided by the Spirit" (Gal 5:16).

Charity is further characterized by unselfishness, initiative, universality, and the gift of oneself to the point of sacrifice.

In loving, a Christian must do as God does: not wait to be loved, but be the first to love. And since he or she cannot do this with God because he is always the first to love, the Christian puts this into practice with each neighbor. St. John tells us that God loves us, but he does not conclude—as would have been more logical—that if God has loved us, we ought to love him in return. Instead he says: "Beloved, if God so loved us, we also ought to love one another" (1 Jn 4:11).

It is only because charity is a participation in God's love (*agape*), that we are able to go beyond natural limits to love our enemies and give our lives for our fellow human beings.

For this reason Christian love rightly belongs to the new era, and the New Commandment is radically new, and introduces something absolutely new into human history and human ethics. "This love," writes Augustine, "makes us new, so that we are new persons, heirs of the New Covenant, singers of the new song."[8]

If Charity is God's love shared with us, it is quite different from philanthropy. In fact, Christian love does not look at people from the point of view of their nature, but from the point of view of God's love for them, because it sees each person as a child of God, as his image.[9]

Likewise, Charity is not mere benevolence. As Leo the Great says: "Earthly benevolence reaches no further than the one it helps. But Christian goodness passes on its Maker," that is, God himself. Therefore, when we do good, we can "be said to be doing good to him who we believe is at work within us."[10]

How charity manifests itself

These lines from the Curé of Ars explain very well how charity manifests itself. They seem to echo Paul's hymn to charity.

> "But," you will say, "how can we know that we have this beautiful and precious virtue, without which our religion is only an illusion?"
>
> First of all, a person who possesses charity is not proud; does not love to dominate others; can never be heard finding fault with others' conduct; does not love to speak about what others are

doing. A person who has charity does not question others' intentions; . . . does not believe he or she can do better than they; does not place himself or herself above his or her neighbor. On the contrary, such a person believes that others always do better, and does not take offence when a neighbor is preferred over him or her. When despised, one who possesses charity remains happy nonetheless, thinking that he or she is deserving of even more contempt.

The person who has charity avoids causing pain to others as much as possible, because charity is a royal mantle which knows well how to hide the mistakes of one's brothers and sisters and never allows itself to think it is better than they are.[11]

According to Vincent de Paul, charity can be expressed by our "making ourselves one" with our neighbor, which has been a characteristic of the Focolare from its earliest years. "To make ourselves one" means to empty ourselves of ourselves in order to understand our neighbor and to put ourselves in his or her situation.

Charity is not being able to see a person suffer without suffering with him or her; or to see someone crying without crying with him or her. It is an act of love which causes hearts to penetrate one another and to feel what the other feels. It is very different from the actions of those people who do not feel anything when they see the torment of the afflicted and the suffering of the poor.

The Son of God had a tender heart. They came to call him to see Lazarus and he went. Mary Magdalen got up and ran out weeping to meet him. The Jews followed her, weeping as well. Everyone was weeping. What did the Lord do? He had so much tenderness and compassion in his soul that he wept with them. It was this tenderness of his which caused him to come down from heaven: he saw the human race deprived of his own glory; he was touched by their misfortune. So we too, like him, must be moved by the sufferings of our neighbor and share his or her sorrow. Oh, Saint Paul, how sensitive you were to these sufferings! Oh, Savior, who filled this apostle with your Spirit and your tenderness, grant that we also may be able to repeat with him: "Who can be sick, and I not sick with him?"

> To be Christians and to see our own brother or sister suffering, and not suffer with him or her, not be sick with him or her, means to be without Charity, to be Christians in name only.[12]

It is evident from listening to these saints that we must love with our whole selves. We cannot love halfway, or without putting our heart into it. Jesus wants a love which, as Luke says, moves us to compassion (cf. Lk 10:33). We must give ourselves totally to our neighbor and receive him or her into our hearts.

If a neighbor wrongs us, we must not answer evil with evil but "overcome evil with good" (Rom 12:21). We must do good to everyone, especially those who share our faith. If we do this, love will more easily become reciprocal. And this mutual love will be of benefit to our brothers and sisters without faith, because it is a witness of God.

Charity, which tends toward reciprocity, has the power to build the Christian community. Paul writes that "love builds up" (1 Cor 8:1), which means that with Christian love we build up the community. And this was the experience of the Focolare at its birth: from isolated members we became a community. It is evident that Christian love was at work in the first Focolarine.

Human beings are not instruments for loving God

Someone might think that in Christianity people could be used as a means for loving God. But that is not so. The theologian Emile Mersch writes:

> Human beings are an end in themselves, an absolute and ultimate value, and mere natural philanthropy can arrive at love for them because of their intrinsic greatness. Could the charity of Christ be less human . . . and fail to discover in the human person more than a mere means for loving God. . . .
> Children can doubtless be happy and proud to be loved for their parents' sake. But this is because they *are* in a way their parents. . . . Yet this should definitely not be the only love they encounter; if it were, they would soon feel not loved, but ignored.

141

Love is truly directed to the person. It does not pass through the person in order to go beyond. What would it be seeking beyond the person? From the moment that the Word became flesh, became one with us (Gal 3:28), we no longer seek God only in far-off heaven, but within each human being as well. He is there . . . as the inner source of life and divinization.[13]

Moreover, the *Pastoral Constitution on the Church in the Modern World* of Vatican II says that "by His incarnation the Son of God has united Himself in some fashion with every human being."[14]

And Catherine of Siena explains what becomes of those who live charity, by revealing to us what the "gentle and loving Word" told her:

Looking at the beauty that I have given the soul, creating it in my image and likeness, observe those who are clothed in the wedding garment of charity, adorned with many real and true virtues, and united to me through love. If you should ask me: "Who are they?" I would answer: "They are another me."[15]

Charity, therefore, divinizes us, makes us sharers in Christ's divinity.

NOTES

Abbreviations

Abbott Walter M. Abbott, editor. *The Documents of Vatican II*. New York, 1966.

PG J. P. Migne. *Patrologiae Cursus Completus Series Graeca*. 162 Vols. Paris, 1857-1866.

PL J. P. Migne. *Patrologiae Cursus Completus Series Latina*. 221 Vols. Paris, 1844-1864.

Part I: When Our Love Is Charity

Mutual Love

1. General Audience, Aug. 12, 1970.
2. *Gaudium et Spes,* 38.

The Name of the Movement is Charity

1. Letter 69, 5.
2. The Lord's Prayer, 23; cf. *Lumen Gentium* 4.
3. *Commentary on the Gospel of John:* first discourse, 1.
4. Letter 14, 4.
5. Sermon 340, 1; quoted by *Lumen Gentium* 32.
6. On Baptism 6.
7. *Gaudium et Spes* 42 and 93.
8. Discourse of Paul VI to the bishops of Australia and the Southern Pacific, Dec. 1, 1970.
9. *Ad Gentes* 22.
10. *Christus Dominus* 28.
11. *Presbyterorum Ordinis* 8.
12. *Christus Dominus* 35.
13. Commentary on the Canticle I, 4.

Part II: Jesus In Our Midst

Where Two or Three Are Gathered in My Name, There Am I in the Midst of Them

1. *Selecta in Jeremiam* 23, 23 (PG 13: 571).
2. *Dem. evang.* 5, 26 (*The Proof of the Gospel*, tr. by W. J. Ferrar [London: S. P. C. K., 1920], Vol I, 268; PG 22: 406-7).
3. *Comm. in Ps.* 84 (PG 23: 1005).
4. *In illud, Vidi Dominum. Hom.* 6, 2 (PG 56: 137).
5. *Contra Celsum* 2, 9 (tr. by Henry Chadwidk [Cambridge University Press, 1953], 74; PG 11; 810).
6. *In Isaiam hom.* 1, 5 (PG 13: 223-4).
7. *In Johannis evangelium* 9 (PG 74: 155).
8. *Comm. in Matth.* 14, 4 (Ante-Nicene Fathers [New York: Charles Scribner's Sons, 1925], Vol. IX, 496; PG 13: 1192).
9. *Enarr. in evang. Matth.* 18, 19-20 (PG 123: 343).
10. *De exhortatione castitatis* 7 (PL 2: 922).
11. *Palamiticarum transgressionum liber* 4, 1 (PG 152: 702).
12. *Comm. in Ps.* 46 (PG 23: 421).
13. *Comm. in Is.* 19 (PG 24: 221).
14. *Apostolic Constitutions* 8, 34 (Ante-Nicene Fathers [New York: Charles Scribner's Sons, 1926], Vol. VII, 496; PG 1: 1138).
15. *De fuga* 14 (PL 2: 120).
16. *Catechetical Sermons* (PG 99: 622).
17. *Festal Epistles* 10, 2 (PG 26: 1397-8).
18. *De unitate ecclesiae* 12 (tr. by Maurice Bévenot, S. J., in Cyprian, *De Lapsis and De Ecclesiae Catholicae Unitate* [Oxford: Clarendon Press, 1971], 77-79; PL 4: 524-5).

The Value of Jesus in Our Midst

1. *In Ecclesiasten* 4 (PG 98: 914).
2. *Practicorum capitum centuria* 1, 77 (PG 120: 887).
3. *Expos in Psalmum* 133 (PG 55: 385).
4. *In Ep. ad Hebr.* 19, 1 (PG 63: 140).
5. *In inscriptionem Actuum Apostolorum* 2, 4 (PG 51: 83).
6. *Regulae brevius tractatae* q. 225 (PG 31: 1231).
7. *In Matth. hom.* 60, 3 (PG 58: 587).
8. *Epist. lib.* ii (PG 99: 1350).
9. *Comm. in Matth.* 14, 1 (PG 13: 1188).
10. *In Canticum Canticorum* 1, 3-4a (*On the Song of Songs*, tr. by R. P.

Lawson; Ancient Christian Writers, No. 26 [Westminster, Md., 1957], pl 76; GCS 8: 102).

11. *Comm. in Matth.* 14, 1 (Ante-Nicene Fathers [New York, 1925], Vol. IX, 495—translation slightly altered; PG 13: 1184-5).

12. *Ibid.*, 495 (PG 13: 1185).

13. *Oratio* 42: *"Supremum vale"* (PG 36: 465-467).

14. *Comm. in Matth.* 13, 15 (Ante-Nicene Fathers [New York, 1925], Vol. IX, 483; PG 13: 1131).

15. *Ibid.*

16. *De Anna sermo* 5, 1 (PG 54: 669).

17. *Expos. in Prophetam Oseam* 1: 10 (PG 126: 587).

A Community Which Has Jesus in Its Midst

1. *In Can. XVII septimi concilii ecumenici* (PG 132: 1134).

2. *De monasteriis laicis non tradendis* 11 (PG 132: 1134).

3. *Vita sancti Gregorii theologi* (PG 35: 259).

4. *The Long Rules* qu. 5, a. 3 (in St. Basil, *Ascetical Works*, tr. by M. Wagner, The Fathers of the Church [New York, 1950], 244; PG 31: 923).

5. *Ibid.* qu. 37a, 4 (Fathers of the Church, 309-10; PG 31: 1014).

6. *Epp.* 97 (in *Letters*, tr. by A. C. Way, The Fathers of the Church [New York, 1951], Vol. I, 215; PG 32: 493).

7. *Monastic Constitutions* 34, 1 (PG 31: 1423-6).

8. *Epist. lib.* ii (PG 99: 1446).

9. *In Ep. II ad Thess. hom.* 4, 4 (PG 62: 491).

10. *Sermon* 132 (in *Saint Peter Chrysologus: Selected Sermons, and Saint Valerian: Homilies*, tr. by George E. Ganss, S. J., Fathers of the Church [New York, 1953], 216; PL 52: 561).

11. *Ibid.* 217 (PL 52: 562).

12. *In Matth. hom.* 60, 2 (PG 58: 587).

13. *Quaestiones* 109 bis (PG 89: 761-4).

Jesus in the Midst and the Life of the Church

1. *Hom.* 2, 9 (*Corpus Christianorum* 122: 240).

2. Teresa Ledochowska, O.S.U., *Il Ceppo dai molti virgulti* (Milano: Ancora, 1972), 187-8.

3. D. Pezeril, *Pauvre et Saint Curé d'Ars* (Paris, 1959), 93.

4. Ste. Therese de l'Enfant Jésus, *Lettres* (Lisieux, 1948), 369.

5. Lemoyne, G. B., *Vita di S. Giovanni Bosco* (Torino: S. E. I., 1962), Vol. II, 140.

6. "Note sul Concilio come assemblea e sulla conciliarità fondamentale della Chiesa," in *Orizonti attuali della teologia* (Rome: Ed. Paoline, 1967), Vol. II, 172-3.

7. *Epp.* 55 (PG 77: 294).
8. *Adv. Jud. oratio* 3 (PG 48: 865).
9. *Contra Monoph.* (PG 86: 1878).
10. *De imag. oratio* (PG 94: 1282).
11. Cf. PL 54: 959.
12. P. Foresi, *Reaching for More* (New York: New City Press, 1972), 71-72.
13. *Constitution on the Sacred Liturgy*, par. 7 (in *Vatican Council II: The Conciliar and Post Conciliar Documents*, Ed. Austin Flannery, O. P. [Collegeville, Minn. : Liturgical Press, 1975], 5).
14. *Decree on the Up-to-date Renewal of Religious Life*, par. 15 (Flannery, 620).
15. *Decree on the Apostolate of Lay People*, par. 17 (Flannery, 784).
16. Par. 18 (Flannery, 785).
17. Pars. 9-11 (Flannery, 776-80).
18. *Decree on Ecumenism*, par. 8 (Flannery, 460-61).
19. *Insegnamenti di Paolo VI* (Tipografia Poliglotta Vaticana, 1965), II, 1072-1074.

Part III: When Did We See You Lord?

Made In God's Image

1. Claus Westermann, *Genesis* I/1 (Neukirchen, 1974): 217-218.
2. Irenaeus, *Against Heresies* IV. 20. 1, in *The Ante-Nicene Fathers* (Grand Rapids, 1969), Vol. I, 487-488 (PG 7, 1032).
3. Gregory of Nyssa, *De hom. opif.* 5 (PG 44, 137).
4. John Chrysostom, Homily III Concerning the Statutes, in *The Nicene and Post-Nicene Fathers* (Grand Rapids, 1956), Vol. IX, 362; PG 49,57.
5. Origen, *In Gen. hom.* XIII. 4 (PG 12, 234).
6. Augustine, *On the Psalms*, translated by Hebgin and F. Corrigan (Westminster, Md., 1960), Vol. I, 47; PL 36, 81.
7. Irenaeus, *Against Heresies* V. 10. 1, in *The Ante-Nicene Fathers* Vol. I (Grand Rapids, 1969): 536; PG 7, 1147-1148.
8. Pope Paul VI, Address of December 8, 1965 at the close of the Second Vatican Council, in *The Teachings of the Second Vatican Council* (Westminster, Md., 1966): 606.
9. Pope Paul VI, Apostolic Exhortation *Marialis Cultus*, par. 57, in *The Teachings of Pope Paul VI*, Vol. 7 (Vatican, 1974): 428.
10. Gottfried Hierzenberger in *Praktisches Bibellexikon*, ed. Anton Grabner—Haider (Freiburg, 1977), col. 740.
11. Walther Eichrodt, *Theology of the Old Testament* (London 1961), Vol. I, 365.
12. Notker Füglister, "Afferrati da Jahwè" in J. Schreiner *et. al.*, *Parola e Messaggio* (Bari, 1970), 222.
13. Otto Kaiser, *Isaiah 1-12: A Commentary* (Philadelphia, 1972) 16.
14. See Claus Westermann, *Isaiah 40-60: A Commentary* (London, 1969). 336-337.

Jesus' Presence In the Christian As Presented In the New Testament

1. Cf. S. Légasse, *Jésus et l'enfant* (Paris, 1969), 72-75.
2. Stanislas Lyonnet, S. J., "The Presence of Christ and His Spirit in Man" in *Concilium* 50 (1969) 101.
3. F. X. Durrwell, *La resurrection de Jésus mystère de salut* 10th (entirely revised) edition (Paris, 1976), 169-170; cf. English translation by Rosemary Sheed of the 2nd French edition: *The Resurrection: A Biblical Study* (New York, 1960). 216-217.
4. M. J. Lagrange, *Evangile selon St. Jean*, 5th ed. (Paris, 1936) 389.

Jesus In Those Who Suffer

1. John Chrysostom, *Homilies on the Gospel of Matthew 88, 3 (PG 58, 778)*.
2. Leo the Great, *Sermons* 10, 2 (PL 54, 165).
3. John Chrysostom, *Matthew* 50, 4 (PG 58, 508-509).
4. Cyprian, *The Dress of Virgins* 11 (PL 4, 461-462).
5. Ambrose, *De Tobia* 16, 55 (PL 14, 781).
6. Ambrose, *Letters* 21, 33 (PL 16, 1017).
7. Augustine, *On the Psalms* 33, 3, 6 (PL 36, 388).
8. Curé of Ars, *Pensieri in Scritti scelti* (Rome, 1975), 83.
9. *Ibid.*, 83.
10. Bonaventure, *Legenda Minor* 7.
11. Raymond of Capua, *The Life of St. Catherine of Siena*, tr. George Lamb (New York, 1960) 121-124 (abridged).
12. M. Auclair, *La parola a San Vincenzo de Paoli* (Rome, 1971), 132.
13. Bonaventure, *Legenda Maior* 1, 5 in *The Soul's Journey to God—The Tree of Life—The Life of St. Francis*, tr. by E. Cousins (New York, 1978), 188-189.
14. Bonaventure, *Legenda Maior* 8, 5 in Cousins, 254.
15. *Insegnamenti di Paolo VI*, II (Vatican, 1965) 1110.
16. *Insegnamenti di Paolo VI*, II (Vatican, 1965) 1178.
17. *Insegnamenti di Paolo VI*, III (Vatican, 1966) 1219-1220.
18. Pope John Paul II, General audience of September 27, 1978, in *The Pope Speaks* 23 (1978) 328.

Christ and the Non-Christians

1. See P. Rossano, "What Vatican Council II has taught regarding non-Christians," *Christ to the World* 12 (1967), 428-436.
2. *Ad Gentes: Decree on the Church's Missionary Activity*, Art. 4, Abbott, 587.
3. *Nostra Aetate: Declaration on the Relationship of the Church to Non-Christian Religions*, Art. 2, Abbott, 662.
4. *Ad Gentes*, Art. 9, Abbott, 595-596.
5. *Nostra Aetate*, Art. 2, Abbott, 662.
6. *Ad Gentes*, Art. 11, Abbott, 598.
7. Justin Martyr, *Second Apology*, 13 (PG 6, 465-468).
8. *Ad Gentes*, Art. 18, Abbott, 607.
9. *Ad Gentes*, Art. 3, Abbott, 586.
10. *Lumen Gentium: Dogmatic Constitution on the Church*, Art. 16, Abbott, 35.
11. See *Ad Gentes*, Art. 9, Abbott, 595-596.
12. See *Nostra Aetate*, Art. 2, Abbott, 662-663.
13. See P. Rossano (above ch. 4, note 1).

14. *Ad Gentes,* Art. 11, Abbott, 598.
15. *Ad Gentes,* Art. 22, Abbott, 612-613.
16. *Sacrosanctum Concilium: Constitution on the Sacred Liturgy,* Art. 37, Abbott, 151.
17. See: *Ad Gentes,* Art. 12, 41, Abbott, 598, 628; *Nostra Aetate,* Art. 2, 5, Abbott, 661, 667; *Unitatis Redintegration: Decree on Ecumenism,* Art. 12, Abbott, 354; *Apostolican Actuositatem: Decree on the Apostolate of the Laity,* Art. 27, Abbott, 515.
18. *Lumen Gentium,* Art. 16, Abbott, 34-35.
19. See *Cristiani e musulmani,* ed. by Secretariat for non-Christians (Bologna, 1970), 36-39.
20. Quotes from the Koran taken from *The Koran,* translated by N. J. Dawood (New York, 1974).
21. See *Cristiani e musulmani,* 71-73.
22. See *Cristiani e musulmani,* 30-32.
23. See R. Arnaldey, "La mystique musulmane" in *La mystique et les mystiques* (Paris, 1975), 579-580.
24. D. Spada, "Induismo" in *Le grandi religioni del mondo* (Rome, 1977), 97-99. Scripture quotes here and in note 26 taken from *Hindu Scriptures,* translated by R. C. Zaehner (London, 1966).
25. P. Rossano, *L'uomo e la religione* (Fossano, 1968).
26. H. Le Saux, "Sagesse Hindoue Mystique Chrétienne du védanta à la Trinité" (Paris, 1965) 217-218; cf. the revised English edition: Abhishiktananda [H. Le Saux], *Saccidananda: A Christian Approach to Advaitic Experience* (Delhi, 1974) 158.
27. H. Le Saux, French ed., 218-219; English ed., 159.
28. See M. Dhavamony, "La ricerca della salvezza nell'Induismo" in *La ricerca della salvezza* (Fossano, 1969), 103.
29. *Nostra Aetate,* Art. 2, Abbott, 661-662.
30. See J. Masson, "Il bene e il male nel buddismo" in *Il bene e il male nelle religioni* (Fossano, 1970), 100-101.
31. See G. Shirieda, "Il buddismo" in *Le religioni non cristiane nel Vaticano II* (Turin, 1966), 144-145.
32. G. Shirieda, 146-148; see J. Masson, 105-106.
33. *Gaudium et Spes: Pastoral Constitution on the Church in the Modern World,* Art. 22, Abbott, 221-222.
34. *Gaudium et Spes,* Art. 22, Abbott, 221; see *Lumen Gentium,* Art. 16, Abbott, 35.
35. See P. Rossano, "What the II Vatican Council has taught regarding non-Christians."
36. *Ad Gentes,* Art. 3, Abbott, 112.
37. *Gaudium et Spes,* Art. 16, Abbott, 213-214.
38. *Ad Gentes,* Art, 12, Abbott, 599.
39. See *Gaudium et Spes,* Art. 16, Abbott, 214.

40. *Gaudium et Spes,* Art. 36, Abbott, 234.
41. *Lumen Gentium,* Art. 16, Abbott, 35.
42. *Traduction Oecumenique de la Bible* (Paris, 1977), note z, 297.
43. *Lumen Gentium,* Art. 48, Abbott, 79.

How To Love Our Neighbor

1. Catherine of Siena, *Dialogo,* 69, in *Il messaggio di Santa Caterina da Siena dottore della Chiesa* (Rome, 1970), 689-690.
2. Gregory the Great, *Morals on the Book of Job* 7, 28 (PL 75, 780-781).
3. Isidore of Seville, *Sententiae* II, 3, 7 (PL 83, 603).
4. Curé of Ars, *Scritti scelti* (Rome, 1975), 114.
5. John of the Cross, quoted in P. Descouvemont, *Sainte Thérèse de l'Enfant Jésus et son prochain* (Paris, 1962), 209.
6. E. Dhanis, "Le message évangélique de l'amour et l'unité de la communauté humaine," *Nouvelle Revue Théologique,* 92 (1970) 186-188.
7. "Amore di Dio e amore del prossimo," in *La Civiltà Cattolica,* 3053 (1977) 346-347.
8. See *Civiltà Cattolica,* 3053 (1977) 351-352.
9. See *Civiltà Cattolica,* 3053 (1977) 349-350.
10. Leo the Great, *Sermons,* 45, 3 (PL 54, 290).
11. *Scritti scelti,* 117.
12. M. Auclair, *La parola a San Vincenzo de'Paoli* (Rome, 1971), 354-355.
13. Emile Mersch, *Morale et Corps Mystique,* 3rd ed. (Paris, 1949), 146-147.
14. *G. S.,* Art. 22, Abbott, 220-221.
15. Catherine of Siena, *Dialogo* 1, in *Il messaggio,* 243.

Also available in the same series from New City Press:

A CALL TO LOVE, Spiritual Writings, Vol. 1

by Chiara Lubich

"Chiara Lubich has established herself as a Christian writer of considerable proportions. Given her prolific literary output it is fitting that New City Press should issue a retrospective series of Lubich's best works, titled Spiritual Writings. The first work in this series *A Call to Love* comprises three of her most popular studies of momentous Christian living: *Our Yes to God* (1980), *The Word of Life* (1974), and *The Eucharist* (1977)."

B.C. Catholic

ISBN 0-911782-70-2, paper, 5 1/8 x 8, 180 pp.

UNITY AND JESUS FORSAKEN

by Chiara Lubich

"Without being simplistic or reductionistic, Lubich challenges [the reader] to focus on Jesus forsaken as the model for unity and the key to living a life of joy. . . . Lubich's essays reflect a balanced spirituality."

Bishop Robert Morneau, Emmanuel Magazine

ISBN 0-911782-53-2, paper, 5 1/8 x 8, 105 pp.

FROM SCRIPTURE TO LIFE

by Chiara Lubich

"Contains commentaries that author Chiara Lubich has written on 12 different 'Words of Life' practiced by the Focolare Movement, which she founded. . . . Each section of the book includes true stories of people who applied the teaching of the Scripture passage."

Catholic News Service

ISBN 0-911782-83-4, paper, 5 1/8 x 8, 112 pp.

MEDITATIONS

by Chiara Lubich   *7th printing*

"[A] collection of brief but intensely meaningful thoughts carefully mined from the scriptures. Chiara helps us to see all the events of our lives as opportunities for our ultimate . . . perfection."

Liguorian

ISBN 0-911782-20-6, paper 5 1/8 x 8, 134 pp.

ON THE HOLY JOURNEY

by Chiara Lubich

"Every two weeks, Chiara Lubich, foundress and president of the Focolare movement, sends out a spiritual message to committed members throughout the world. This is a collection of those meditations, the principal focus of which is a call to live out the 'holy journey' toward Christian perfection in the world by 'walking together' in the love of Jesus and Mary."

Spiritual Book News

ISBN 0-911782-60-5, paper, 5 1/8 x 8, 166 pp.

DIARY 1964/65

by Chiara Lubich

"Add Chiara Lubich's name to the list of extraordinary Catholic women. . . . In 1964 and 1965 Chiara Lubich made several trips to North and South America to encourage the Focolarini who were establishing their work in the U.S., Argentina, and Brazil. Lubich's diary records her experiences and thoughts during these journeys."

New Oxford Review

ISBN 0-911782-55-9, paper, 5 1/8 x 8, 188 pp.

UNITY—OUR ADVENTURE

The Focolare Movement

This publication tells the story of an adventure: that of the Focolare movement. The book intends to offer a quick panorama of the Focolare's spirituality and history. It contains 40 color and 47 black and white photos.

ISBN 0-911782-56-7, cloth, large format, 80 pp.

STARS AND TEARS

by Michel Pochet

Through a series of interviews with Chiara Lubich, the author traces the development and the spirituality of the Focolare. The style and format is accessible to everyone.

ISBN 0-911782-54-0, paper, 5 1/8 x 8, 153 pp.